INTERNATIONAL TRADE

INTERNATIONAL TRADE

A MANAGEMENT GUIDE

Harold J. Heck

American Management Association

International standard book number: 0-8144-5224-8
Library of Congress catalog card number: 76-173317
First printing

Preface

In the postwar period so much interest has been given to the broader dimensions of international business (which are largely the result of spectacular increases in overseas investments and licensing) that the fundamental of international trade has at times been put in the shadows. Yet the volume of world trade has increased beyond many expectations of even a few years ago. The International Monetary Fund reported that the total of world exports, excluding those of the Soviet Union and Cuba, reached $278 billion in 1970, an increase of 14 percent over the preceding year. At the *same time, imports, which were valued c.i.f. (that is, cost, insurance, and freight to the country of destination), totaled $288 billion. This large increase over the preceding year is not just a flash-in-the-pan performance; in each of the preceding five years the increase was on the order of 10 to 11 percent.*

However, the significant point for our purpose is not the statistical dimension, but the fact that this business must be and will be done by someone. It may be by a private merchant or entrepreneur; it may be by an investor selling to or buying from himself or related person (corporate affiliate, for example) across national boundaries; a government monopoly or state-trading operation may be one of the principals; or part of the trade may be government-generated, that is, the result of foreign aid or of subsidy or subsidy-like assistance to one of the traders.

Little of what has been accomplished in the expansion of international trade could have come about without a conscious and concerted effort on the part of governments to permit and even to encourage their citizens to trade with each other. These attitudes were given substance by laws and regulations and by the governments' participation in international efforts to bring about conditions under which trade opportunities could be sought out and cultivated without unnecessary political impediments. The United States' trade agreements program is a positive channel marker, as are its extensive and aggressive trade promotion programs, which include both passive and active promotional efforts. In addition, the U.S. government, like many others, offers certain export incentives that are consistent with its position in a number of international organizations. The final chapter outlines U.S. government attitudes toward exporting and importing.

On a bilateral and multilateral basis the U.S. government has negotiated treaties and agreements pertaining to the right of its citizens to do business abroad and assuring nondiscriminatory treatment for them. At the same time, the most-favored-nation concept in international trading relationships has lost much of its meaning because of both authorized and unauthorized deviations from it. ("Authorized" means agreed to by the countries against which the discrimination is effective; agreement comes about primarily through customs unions and free trade associations.)

In spite of this deviation from the nondiscriminatory trading concept of the last few decades, international trade has vastly expanded, and a number of international organizations are dedicated to a continued expansion of trading opportunities. Among these are the General Agreement on Tariffs and Trade (GATT), the Organization for Economic Cooperation and Development (OECD), and the International Monetary Fund (IMF), all of which are positively oriented toward an expanding volume of international trade. The United States plays a dominant role in all of them.

This book has been designed primarily for the private practitioner of exporting and importing, whether he is doing business with a private and independent trader or his own subsidiary abroad, or with a foreign government or other public-sector trading unit. The technical and procedural aspects are presented primarily from the viewpoint of a private businessman. Hence no attention is given to the unique problems of East-West trading opportunities and practices, although these will undoubtedly be an interesting development in the future, nor to selling to or buying from foreign governments or quasi-governmental units. These present a type of business challenge different from the kind one faces in conducting trade through private hands, especially in matters such as distribution channels, foreign market development, and financing.

In the preparation of this book questions arose as to the place of exporting in the multinational firm. Little could be done with this subject because the determining factor is each firm's organization for international operations. In some cases, companies will be organized along a product-line division of responsibility and that responsibility may be worldwide. In other cases, they may be organized geographically. In others, a centralized export function may be all-encompassing in responsibility, in terms of both geography and products, but naturally with required coordination within the overall parent organizational structure.

Whatever the form of internal organization involved in moving goods across national boundaries, the functions, procedures, and technical considerations are substantially the same. So are government policies and regulations, except perhaps where a type of legal organization is permitted or provided for because of tax or restrictive business implications. For that reason, emphasis has been placed on such technical and procedural considerations rather than on organization itself.

Finally, no matter who the principals in the transactions are, the greatly expanded volume of international trade is of direct importance to ports and port operations, international transportation companies, commercial banks with foreign departments, marine insurance companies, foreign freight forwarders, customs brokers, and many other services that enter into the complexity of moving goods across national frontiers. The role of these supporting services necessarily underlies the chapters on technical and procedural aspects and on the financing of exports and imports.

Harold J. Heck

Contents

1

International Trade and the National Economy

International trade has some impact on everyone's life and is significant to the nation as a whole for both economic and political reasons. It is vital to the American economy and to employment opportunities, and fundamental to such international specialization of labor as can be enjoyed in a world whose nations' physical boundaries are in some cases illogical, where nationalistic feelings rest at times on overcharged emotionalism, and where political units must strive deliberately for short-term, if not immediate, economic betterment in order to maintain a semblance of political stability.

In 1970, exports from the United States, excluding military grant aid, were $43 billion, and imports were $40 billion. Thus, $83 billion worth of merchandise moved across our borders in one year, an increase of 55 percent in exports over 1965, and an increase of close to 90 percent in imports. Over and above the figures for merchandise transactions, American direct investments abroad as of year-end 1969 were estimated at $71 billion. Interest, dividends, branch earnings, and fees and royalties from these direct investments amounted to $7.9 billion in 1970. However, let us limit our view to trade in merchandise.

Relationship of Exports to GNP

The most widely used and broadest economic statistic in any country is probably its gross national product (GNP), the statistic by which economic growth is commonly measured. A breakdown of the economic sectors that yield or encourage the growth of GNP reveals some interesting comparisons of the relative importance that international markets have for a nation's production.

In the United States, exports of merchandise have consistently run around 4 or 5 percent of GNP over a 20-year period. This small percentage suggests that foreign trade—and here we mean exports—does not have as great an impact on the overall economy as it does in certain other countries. The ratio of exports to GNP for a selected list of countries is given in Table 1. Obviously, all these countries must rely on foreign demand to absorb their output to a greater extent than the United States. The United Kingdom, which sells about 16 percent of its output to foreigners, pointed up this reliance a few years ago when it adopted the slogan, "Export or Die." Consider how much more dependent on foreign trade is a country like Belgium or the Netherlands or Kuwait. And consider, especially, how this dependence takes a strong social and political coloration when the output is concentrated in one or in very few products.

It is obvious that a nation's dependence on export markets must influence the attitudes of its people and the policies of its government, and hence its international relations. Moreover, it is bound to influence a nation's position in international organizations that are concerned with either economic or political relations, a factor of particular significance when the one-nation, one-vote policy prevails, as it does in many of the international bodies to which the United States is party. In other words, these varying de-

Table 1. Exports in relation to gross national product for selected countries.

Country	*Year*	*Percent of Exports to GNP*
Mexico	1968	5
Brazil	1968	5
Colombia	1968	8
Argentina	1969	8
Japan	1969	10
France	1969	11
Philippines	1969	11
Italy	1969	14
Australia	1969	14
Chile	1966	14
Guatemala	1968	15
United Kingdom	1969	16
Peru	1969	17
Austria	1969	19
Germany	1968	19
Sweden	1968	19
Canada	1969	20
Denmark	1969	22
Norway	1969	23
Costa Rica	1969	23
Switzerland	1968	23
Venezuela	1968	31
Netherlands	1969	35
Belgium	1968	39
Kuwait	1968	63

SOURCE: Developed from data in *International Financial Statistics,* January 1971, International Monetary Fund, Washington, D.C.

grees of dependence on foreign trade affect our own international relations.

Exports and Production of Movable Goods

As interesting as the ratio of exports to GNP of any country is, that ratio is really not a good measure of the importance of foreign demand to a nation's economic activity. It is not a valid measure because GNP—the base against which the comparison is made—includes many components that could not possibly be exported.

For example, it includes the year's estimated cost of construction of streets and highways, naturally not exportable. The same holds for other construction, such as bridges, dams, factories, public utilities, airports, ports and harbors, private homes, theaters, stadiums, and services performed within the country—none of which are intended for export. The ratio of exports to the production of movable goods is a much more meaningful indication of the quantitative significance of foreign trade to an economy. The Department of Commerce estimates that for the United States this ratio is on the order of 9 percent.

A company's profits are not made on the first few percentage points of sales, wherever made, but on the last. The first part of a period's sales brings in income to cover both fixed and variable costs, and only after fixed costs for the period are covered can profits be anticipated. To the extent that volume based on foreign demand is used in costing and pricing for export, the fixed costs attributable thereto are actually absorbed and the opportunity for profit becomes more real. Only after all costs are absorbed, however, and not just programmed on average, can profit be anticipated and realized. Hence profit comes from the top percentages of total sales, and these are the base for profitable operations. Therefore, if 8 or 10 percent of sales abroad are chopped off or reduced substantially, the profit anticipation on which investment and production were based stands to be seriously affected. Without this anticipation, investment, employment, and production would have to be cut back, or at least would not be called forth.

Exports and Commodity and Product Sectors

The impact of foreign trade on the economy and on citizens can readily be demonstrated by relating exports to output of specific segments of production. This brings the picture home to individual businesses, where dollar volume is an important consideration.

Table 2 shows the percentages of production of selected product groupings that were exported in 1967. Apparent are interesting dispersions from an overall average of 9 or 10 percent based on exports of more than $14 billion—about a third of total U.S. exports for the year. In a third of the product groupings over 20 percent of production was absorbed by foreign demand, and in several over 33 percent went to foreign markets. Thus export trade means a great deal more to certain product sectors of the economy

Table 2. Exports in relation to production in 1967 for selected products.

	Production Exported (%)	*Value of Exports ($ million)*
Raw cotton	49	464
Corn	14	704
Grain sorghums	40	299
Soybeans	32	772
Leaf tobacco	37	487
Fresh fruits	10	155
Bituminous coal and lignite	19	475
Phosphate rock	36	94
Sulfur	32	82
Hides, skins, and pelts	45	127
Dry milk products	15	95
Milled rice and byproducts	58	315
Soybean oil mill products	18	320
Grease and inedible tallow	50	153
Pulp mill products	28	248
Paperboard, except wet machine board	8	211
Cyclic coal tar intermediates	14	150
Industrial inorganic chemicals not elsewhere classified	11	388
Plastic materials, synthetic resins, and nonvulcanized elastomers	10	448
Synthetic rubber	17	170
Medicinals and botanicals	36	197
Fertilizers	9	142
Lubricating oils and greases	19	247
Refined copper	20	160
Valves and pipe fittings	9	194
Steam engines, turbogenerators, and parts	10	104
Farm machinery	11	458
Construction and mining machinery and equipment	28	1,190
Oil-field machinery	32	208
Machine tools, metal cutting type	11	199
Food products machinery	18	125
Textile machinery	19	125
Special industry machinery	22	354
Pump and compressors	17	331
Electronic computing equipment	11	432

Table 2 (Continued)

	Production Exported (%)	*Value of Exports ($ million)*
Electric measuring instruments	14	164
Radio and television broadcast equipment	26	91
Solid-state semiconductor devices	12	152
Truck tractors, truck chassis, and trucks	10	429
Aircraft	13	1,089
Aircraft engines and engine parts	9	323
Aircraft parts and auxiliary equipment not elsewhere classified	12	588
Locomotives and parts	18	103
Scientific and mechanical measuring instruments, and automatic temperature controls	16	460
Photographic equipment and supplies	10	323

SOURCE: U.S. Bureau of the Census, *U.S. Commodity Exports–Imports as Related to Output, 1967 and 1966*, Table 2A, September 1970.

than it does to others. This touches on the matter of geographic impact and employment.

Geographic Source of Exports

Another interesting and meaningful indicator of the significance of foreign trade to the American economy is to be found in identifying the origin of exports within the United States. Because the shipper's export declarations no longer require that the state of origin of the exported product be shown (a detail discontinued in the early 1930s), the desired information had to be obtained from a special survey conducted by the Department of Commerce.

The first of some recent surveys was for 1960. Subsequent surveys were made for 1963, 1966, and 1969. These surveys cover exports of manufactured goods only and are based on responses to questionnaires sent to manufacturers that have 100 or more employees and that export as much as $25,000 per year. Responses to the 1969 survey showed that 10,660 plants had export shipments of $25,000 or more. This makes the survey detailed and comprehensive indeed, but it does not give as complete or precise a measure of geographic dependence on foreign markets as might be desired because it omits agricultural and mineral exports, which are an important part of the total and a still more important element for certain sections of the country.

However, estimates of state participation in exports of agricultural products are made by the Department of Agriculture. These are derived mainly by allocating to each state a share of total exports based on the state's contribution to the nation's output of agricultural products as shown by cash receipts from farm marketings. Thus the figures represent exports that might be attributed to each state rather than be recorded in the export process.

Of course the survey of exports of manufactured goods has certain shortcomings. For example, components may have been produced in one state and incorporated into a product reported as an export from another state.

Another qualification is possible inaccuracy due to lack of coverage or response and to the fact that respondent data had to be blown up to indicate state proportions of a national total. To that extent there will be some possibility of error. (The manufacturing establishments reporting in the survey for 1969 accounted for $20 billion, or 70 percent, of all U.S. exports of manufactured products in 1969. The balance, exported through wholesalers or other purchasers whose intention to export was not known to the manufacturers, and by small manufacturers not covered in the survey, was allocated by the Census Bureau.)

These reservations are not to be taken as critical of the methodology or even as casting doubt on the validity of the ultimate data. However, in using statistics, one must realize that because of inaccuracies or shortcomings in basic data, fine computations or comparisons based on statistics should be used with caution. Nevertheless, for its purpose, the survey of exports of manufactured goods is excellent, and certainly the best available source. It facilitates an understanding at grass-roots level of the dependence of nations on foreign markets for the sale of their products and for jobs arising therefrom.

The data, in spite of certain shortcomings, serve several important functions. For example, they make it easier for newspapers and other information media to bring to the public the meaning of foreign markets in a way that can be properly understood. They also give legislators and other government officials a body of reference material that better enables them to take informed positions on foreign trade legislation and policy. Moreover, they provide these legislators and officials with reasonably indicative facts so that they can deal with special interest pressures that, if honored, could have a negative effect on other identifiable, but perhaps not organized, local economic interests.

Table 3 shows that exports of manufactured goods in 1969 came from every state, that 37 states can be said to have relied on foreign markets for more than $100 million of their production, and that eight states provided well over $1 billion each of exports to

Table 3. Apparent source of exports in 1969, by state ($ million).

State	*Manufactures*	*Agricultural Products* *	State	*Manufactures*	*Agricultural Products*
Alabama	318	60	Montana	14	80
Alaska	(25–50)	0	Nebraska	101	270
Arizona	157	62	Nevada	(10–25)	1
Arkansas	204	296	New Hampshire	74	— †
California	2,720	556	New Jersey	1,114	16
Colorado	157	69	New Mexico	16	20
Connecticut	659	3	New York	2,296	39
Delaware	124	19	North Carolina	739	406
Florida	426	126	North Dakota	7	195
Georgia	428	106	Ohio	2,338	205
Hawaii	(10–25)	19	Oklahoma	158	115
Idaho	35	64	Oregon	241	42
Illinois	2,343	650	Pennsylvania	1,902	53
Indiana	999	305	Rhode Island	110	— †
Iowa	412	505	South Carolina	254	118
Kansas	241	314	South Dakota	13	87
Kentucky	345	92	Tennessee	472	104
Louisiana	396	154	Texas	1,468	422
Maine	77	3	Utah	48	10
Maryland	362	40	Vermont	52	2
Massachusetts	818	3	Virginia	581	88
Michigan	2,613	94	Washington	955	107
Minnesota	492	276	West Virginia	235	3
Mississippi	181	158	Wisconsin	785	71
Missouri	634	216	Wyoming	(1–5)	5

SOURCE: Manufactures: U.S. Bureau of the Census, *Current Industrial Reports Series MA-161(60)-2, Survey of the Origin of Exports by Manufacturing Establishments: 1969*, 1970. Agricultural products: U.S. Department of Agriculture, *Foreign Agricultural Trade of the United States*, October 1970.

* Year ending June 30, 1970 for agricultural products.
† Less than 1.

foreign markets. What may be somewhat of a surprise is the extent to which states in the interior of the country are significant exporters of manufactured goods.

The table also incorporates attributed state shares in U.S. exports of agricultural commodities. These estimates, in conjunction with the export interest based on manufactured goods, demonstrate that foreign demand influences every section of the country. Hence, the meaning of dependence on foreign markets is brought nearer home; and if keeping our own domestic markets open to foreigners so they can earn the dollars with which to pay for our exports is brought into question, it becomes more obvious that losses of foreign markets could play a damaging role in many local areas within the United States.

Exports and Employment

Along with the impact of exports on the balance of payments, which statistics make so clearly visible, one of the most meaningful facts about exports is that they mean production, and production means jobs.

Estimates of the number of jobs traceable to exports have been made by the Department of Labor for 1966. The results were published in the *Monthly Labor Review* for June 1969. In summary, it was estimated that about 2.5 million jobs in the United States were related to U.S. exports of merchandise. This includes both primary employment in industries actually producing exports and indirect employment in industries supplying goods and services used in producing the exports. In addition, another 600,000 jobs were said to be based on the export of services, such as sales of transportation and other services to foreigners, and receipts from foreign travel in the United States.

The estimates suggest that exports provided 507,000 jobs in agriculture, forestry, and fisheries, 58,000 in mining, 1,203,000 in manufacturing, 633,000 in various services directly connected with the export of goods from the United States, and 34,000 in government. Table 4 breaks these totals down to industries.

Exports and Individual Companies

Like domestic business, international business is conducted by companies and individuals, not by industries or other broad economic sectors. So, although tabulations of industry and product dependence on foreign markets are revealing, a clearer picture of the

Table 4. Employment in selected manufacturing industries attributable to exports in 1966 (in thousands).

Industry	*Estimated Export Employment*	
Food and kindred products		56
Apparel		16
Lumber and wood products		41
Chemicals		67
Rubber and miscellaneous plastic products		33
Primary iron and steel manufacturing		82
Primary nonferrous metals manufacturing		42
Heating, plumbing, and structural metal products		19
Machinery		357
Engines and turbines	17	
Farm machinery and equipment	17	
Construction, mining, and oil-field machinery	46	
Metalworking machinery and equipment	36	
Office, computing, and accounting machines	19	
Electrical industrial equipment and apparatus	37	
Radio, television, and communication equipment	28	
Electronic components and accessories	25	
Motor vehicles and equipment	48	
Aircraft and parts	65	
Scientific and controlling instruments	29	

SOURCE: "Report on Employment Related to Exports," *Monthly Labor Review*, June 1969, p. 16.

foreign trade impact could emerge if individual *company* dependence on exports and imports were known. However, such data are not required to be reported to government agencies or to be published for stockholders, so the only source would be a special survey. In the preparation of this text, the author asked 25 large American companies what proportion of sales from domestic facilities went to export. For this purpose, Canada was to be considered as a foreign market, even though some companies treat it as domestic, administratively.

All these companies had international divisions, which implies manufacturing abroad, directly or under license, so exports from the United States should be expected to be a small part of their U.S. production. The percentages ranged from 1 to 24 percent. Over half the respondents reported that exports were less than 10 percent of sales from domestic (United States) facilities. Perhaps company dependence on exports is not as meaningful as some other quantifications, since many companies produce in more than one plant, often in several states and in different parts of the country.

In their annual reports to stockholders, many companies show a figure or two pertaining to their international operations. The detail depends in part on the accounting method used for consolidating all operations, domestic and foreign. Typically, the key figures one desires for comparative purposes are the percentage of earnings traceable to foreign operations (in which earnings on exports from the United States are or should be included) and the percentage of sales traceable to foreign operations.

For some years, *Business International* has tabulated and published such data for several companies, usually arranged in broad industry groupings. Table 5 shows the data for a few selected companies for 1969. The data given pertain to all international opera-

Table 5. Importance of international operations to earnings and sales of selected companies in 1969.

Company	*Percent Foreign to Total*	
	Net Assets	*Earnings*
Black & Decker	39	46
Chrysler	22	21
Goodyear	38	31
International Harvester	27	27
Otis Elevator	39	49
IBM	28	43
Mobil Oil	44	44
Standard Oil (N.J.)	49	48
Dow Chemical	26	40
Eastman Kodak	22	18
American Standard	37	42
National Cash Register	38	63
Woolworth	46	59
Gillette	49	45
Johnson & Johnson	22	34
Pfizer	51	51
Squibb	41	66
CPC International	56	50
H. J. Heinz	52	50
Honeywell	27	21

SOURCE: *Business International,* various issues from July 3 to Oct. 30, 1970.

NOTE: Some company data include Canadian figures in U.S. data; some exclude unconsolidated subsidiaries; some specifically state "includes U.S. exports," so the presumption must be that some may not show exports from the U.S. as "foreign sales" or earnings from exports as "foreign earnings."

tions of the companies shown and not just to their exports. And it is evident that international business is concerned with more than international trade; it involves manufacturing abroad and under license, as well as exporting and importing.

With a third to a half, and sometimes more, of earnings attributed to international operations, it is easy to understand the interest in jobs, the great recruitment activity of many companies, and the rapid and widespread expansion in the offering of international business programs in many colleges and universities. The companies identified in Table 5 are all large, and export and import opportunities are certainly not limited to companies such as these. In recent years there have been exhortations, especially by the government, for more people to go into export because of balance of payments pressures. A recent secretary of commerce used a pet statistic to the effect that only 4 to 5 percent of American businesses were in export, and he would have liked the figure to be closer to 10 percent.

Actually, we do not know how many companies are actively engaged in export. There is no official figure on this, because no license or registration is required. It might be possible to isolate names of exporters from shippers' export declarations when processing statistical data from them, but as far as can be determined, this has not been done. Within the last five years, the Department of Commerce developed the *American International Traders Index*, to be used mainly in embassies and consulates abroad in referring inquiries for potential American exports and in the Department of Commerce's own export promotion program. Some 370,000 letters were sent out to business firms asking if they were engaged in or were interested in exporting. About 70,000 replied in the affirmative and were asked to register in the *American International Traders Index*. As of early 1971, between 20,000 and 25,000 had done so.

Location of Foreign Trade Employment

The objective of several of the foregoing arrangements of foreign trade statistics is the presentation of foreign trade as a live, large, pervasive economic activity of immediate consequence to many of our citizens. To the country as a whole this means several things, but to companies it means opportunity and competition; to individuals it means primarily employment and income.

Anyone contemplating a career in or related to international business must expect to have to seek a job in the private sector, either in the United States or abroad, or in a government agency concerned with international business, again, here or abroad. Many people are attracted by the glamour of foreign trade, understandably so because it suggests travel and living abroad. It comes as something of a surprise, however, to realize that most jobs for Americans in foreign trade are right here in the United States; and a large number are in interior cities rather than in New York, New Orleans, or San Francisco.

One of the best indications of this is the tabulation of export origin by state (Table 3). But the fact that production for export originates in a given state does not mean that the actual conduct of international trade takes place there or that this is the point of contact with the foreign market. For example, an exporter in Philadelphia could be handling exports of goods made in New Jersey or in other parts of the United States. However, a good indication of where foreign trade activity is located is the existence of export managers' clubs, foreign trade clubs, or foreign departments of chambers of commerce. These exist in almost every major city and are also to be found in Bridgeport, Conn., Jacksonville, Florida, Reading, Pa., Grand Rapids, Mich., and Richmond, Va., because that is where the export managers are located. Obviously much of the employment opportunity in foreign trade is to be found in these cities.

Furthermore, some 200 commercial banks, located in 30 states, report short-term claims on foreigners in amounts exceeding $500,000 each. A large part of this represents claims arising from the financing of exports for their customers, so it indicates an active participation in foreign trade at the local level. In fact, the Bankers Association for Foreign Trade has more than 130 members, located in many sections of the country.

In summary, the impact of foreign trade on the economy is significant overall—by industry, by product, by geographic region, and in terms of employment. (Our dependence on foreign sources of supply will be discussed in the chapter on importing.) Many of these relationships are more or less quantifiable, which clarifies the meaning of foreign trade to the economy.

But we should not leave the subject without recognizing that in terms of economic impact a number of nonmeasurable, or qualitative, phenomena are bound to have significant bearing. Some may be said to be advantageous, some perhaps disadvantageous. Among the advantages are:

1. Increased employment, called forth to satisfy actual or anticipated foreign demand.

2. Lower costs for decreasing-cost items, and lower prices because of added volume undertaken to satisfy foreign demand. Lower prices themselves force the weeding out of inefficient producers and provide the basis of a higher standard of living for a greater number of people.
3. Wider markets than may exist domestically, which give rise to more opportunity and diversification.
4. Exports help pay for imports, some of which are not producible at all in a given country and some of which are not producible competitively in volume, quality, and price.
5. Pressure on government policymakers for more flexibility and less rigidity in making economic adjustments that may be politically sensitive.

The disadvantages of foreign trade are more difficult to find, and the concept of disadvantage may hinge on one's economic philosophy, whether market-oriented or socialistic. However, among the disadvantages occasionally cited are:

1. Dependence on economic conditions abroad, both for markets to absorb production and for sources of supply.
2. The propensities of foreign governments to change their commercial policies with little or no warning to foreigners linked through trade with their economies.
3. Interference of international market forces with economic plans and employment programs of government, such as certain agricultural or social undertakings.
4. Pressure by international market forces on high and rigid wage contracts, considered desirable by the beneficiaries but not by consumers, who are forced to pay higher prices.
5. The exhaustion of irreplaceable natural resources through exports.
6. The pressure of competition on prices and on the marginal and submarginal producers and employees.

2

Company and Product Considerations

Usually a company thinks about reaching into foreign markets because it finds itself with unused capacity, unused resources, or, in economic jargon, it is not operating to its margin. It is facing the need or desire to expand operations, so it must look for wider markets, here or abroad. The stage now has been reached for making some decisions. Is export worth the effort? How much effort can be given? How soon? These decisions cannot be haphazard or simply based on hunches. Sometimes they may be, but when one has his money on the line or is handling other peoples' money, such decisions call for cold, hard facts—as many as one can get.

Two reasons why so much attention has been given to this topic in the last decade are the exhortation by government to go into exports because of balance of payments developments, and the establishment of a number of policies and institutional aids to encourage and assist in export attractiveness. Let us say that a company has been attracted by the publicity and decides to give it a try. What must its management think about in making its decision? One consideration is that exporting provides an opportunity for larger markets in which to sell. Another is that it offers a chance to spread overhead and expand production, and thus to take advantage of lower unit costs and increasing profits (sometimes referred to as *economies of scale*).

Requirements of Expansion

A businessman must think and act within the context of his own business structure, however. He will realize that with the passage of time, he will always need cash and working capital to replenish merchandise that is sold and to pay maturing debts and meet other current operating expenses. In a T-account presentation, the structure would be something like this:

Assets	*Liabilities*
Cash	Notes payable to bank
Receivables	Payables to trade creditors
Merchandise	Other short-term debt, including taxes, wages and salaries, interest and other current operating expenses *
Plant	Noncurrent debt
Other fixed assets	Net worth

* Not typically appearing on a balance sheet but included here because they represent the principal ongoing and constant outflow of funds.

Investigating the attractiveness or possibility of exporting calls for the same type of thinking that is required in considering any serious expansion of one's business. It may require new facilities, enlarged or increased resources, and additional manpower. These additional assets can be brought into focus by relating them to certain operational aspects of the business. Moreover, one or more people in the company must change their thinking to a wider, broader base—they may have to move away from the domestic market entirely. Relating these resources to functional or operational demands, we might come up with the following considerations:

Production. If the foreign markets are to be added to the domestic markets now being supplied, can current production lines be maintained and utilized for goods destined for export, or will they have to be changed? What would be involved in a change—new designs, modifications?

Sales volume. What additional sales are anticipated? Can the required goods be provided by present production facilities? Can the added volume be handled by the present distribution setup? Can the present sales manager take on an additional big territory?

New functions. Because of different operational procedures, different laws and regulations, and the different environments faced in foreign markets, one is obliged to deal with new and varied documents, transportation methods and rates, packaging, insurance, advertising, taxation, and possibly with translation requirements. The question is whether present personnel can handle all these matters or whether it will be necessary to hire specialists or farm out some of the responsibilities for a fee.

Management. No business, least of all international business, runs by itself. So here the question is whether present management is in a position to give both domestic and foreign operations all the attention they need. And this, of course, presumes that management is able to handle what may well be a wide range of new and perplexing problems.

Finances. In order to satisfy expanded markets, it will be necessary to carry additional inventory, either because of larger volume or because of the wider variety resulting from modifications to satisfy foreign demand. Furthermore, additional receivables based on credit sales abroad will be called for. This, too, could be because of the larger volume of business but also because of longer credit terms and possibly slower collection than on domestic sales. Therefore a prime question is whether the company has adequate finances for handling this enlargement of assets or whether it is in a position to borrow the funds.

In any case, the foregoing considerations are minimal, so we can see that one cannot just wake up one fine morning and say, "We're going into exporting." Company officers must ask themselves what the company's ultimate intent is. What is its motive? Why go into exporting when, nine times out of ten, the domestic market is so important and in many cases it has not been fully developed?

The Company

There are two major determinants to be most seriously considered at this time: the company and the product. The company can be compared to a table standing on three legs: without any one of them it would fall. These three are:

Men. Export activity means divided interests between the domestic and foreign markets; and it calls for competence, training, and specialization in both domestic and foreign business.

Capital. Expansion means need for more funds to obtain working capital for carrying larger inventory, larger receivables, and probably longer credit terms on receivables.

Physical plant and facilities. Here the need for added facilities (plant or tools, machinery, and equipment) may simply spring from increased volume to supply an expanded market or from modifications in a product that is now to supply more than the domestic market.

Added to these basic components are the company's goodwill, location, and industrial property rights and technology (commonly referred to as patents, trademarks, and know-how), all of which contribute to turn out a product that is unique, or that is similar to others but more attractive, better presented, or produced more efficiently and cheaply, so that the company has a competitive advantage over others seeking to capture the same market.

Importance of the Product

As long as a market is open to supply from competing sources, the most generously financed and technically competent business could fail if what it makes and sells is not exactly what the market wants. As Robert Douglass Stuart stated, "If we are to be more than a supplemental supplier to a market, if we wish to compete effectively, our product cannot be *almost* what the market wants; it must be *just* what the market wants." [1]

Competition is constantly trying to offer a product that is more appealing to a prospective purchaser. This is the fundamental requirement of a product—that it be appealing or useful to prospective buyers. And this holds for imports as well as exports. Domestic producers are constantly faced with the prospect that some producer located elsewhere, possibly in a foreign country, may introduce into the domestic market a new product or an old one that differs from his but is able to compete for his customers.

An American producer may attempt to enter a new foreign

---

[1] *Penetrating the International Market* (New York: American Management Association, 1965), p. 12.

market with a product new to it or, if not new to that particular market, sufficiently different from what the market is accustomed to in order to raise the question of whether his product can satisfy demand in one or more foreign markets. He should consider whether demand can even be stimulated. In other words, is the product exportable?

The fact is that all products for which there is or can be an effective demand satisfy a desire, human or industrial. There must be a market abroad for one's product, or at least sufficient chance of finding and developing one, to justify the export effort. Demand in foreign—potential export—markets varies by age and income group, geographic region, climate, and seasonal change, just as it does in the United States. Similarly, just as there is a difference in the kind of product demanded by consumers and by agricultural or industrial users in the United States, so there is a difference in countries or localities abroad, depending in large part on geographic conditions and on the degree of industrial development there.

In large measure what is useful and demanded in one country is useful and demanded in at least some others. Some modification or special design or color may be called for to conform to local preferences, but this is the very essence of demand satisfaction. The story goes that one of the pioneers in the automobile industry said, "Sure, you can have your car in any color you like—as long as it is black." On that one little point alone, competition saw to it that the consumer's preferences had to be met to win his favor.

One question for a producer considering exporting, then, is: Is my product exportable as-is or with this or that modification for this or that market? This presumes that the company is able to offer its output at a price that is bearable in the foreign market. It also presumes that a potential exporter will see enough light at the end of the tunnel to justify the expenditure of time and money necessary to identify a few foreign markets (assuming he has the productive capacity to satisfy more than one market) and to do the necessary detailed study of the selected markets on which to base a decision as to which ones, when, in what volumes, and so on.

When one or more countries are selected for attention, a potential exporter must try to get the dimensions of the isolated market, with the product as-is, for economies of scale; this means without major modification, if any at all. He will want to know who uses similar products in that country, who buys them, and where. The product itself will narrow consideration to a number of countries by ruling some out entirely.

Product Analysis

Evaluating a product made primarily for domestic markets in terms of its appeal abroad calls for objective thinking. Let us refer to this as *product analysis*, which involves such considerations as:

- Recognizing what the product does and what needs it satisfies.
- Identifying the features that differentiate one's product: sizes, optional offerings, ranges of quality, operating conditions and restrictions.
- Understanding what a consumer needs in order to use it: skills, complementary technology (such as other equipment).
- Recognizing the cost of operating the product (fuel, power, maintenance).
- Determining the seasonality of product usefulness, and shelf life.
- Estimating servicing requirements (repairs and spare parts).
- Relating the impact of taste, style, custom, or religious preference to a product's size, color, shape, ingredients, taste, and packaging.

These considerations suggest that product analysis involves an examination of consumer needs in different environments as well as the identification of new customers, with varying habits and characteristics, in unfamiliar foreign environments. The question really is, what kind of consumer is our product likely to appeal to, and how can he be identified—anywhere?

Discussion of the product in this context assumes, as stated by Stuart, that

> When, however, the decision has been made to expand, to take an important share of the available foreign markets—when the profit potential has become clear—we must be ready to make some changes in our product, its packaging, and in fact our whole marketing approach. If the job of analyzing market opportunities has been intelligently carried out, we know the probable potential. No longer will we be satisfied to accept whatever sales can be made through our agents; from now on, our goal will be to achieve what we see as our potential.[2]

In all this, it is necessary first to look at a product from the buyer's point of view. Hence, Root's idea of concentric aspects of a product, which bring into account the physical core; the product

[2] Stuart, p. 40.

package, including the brand name and trademark; and auxiliary services such as performance guarantees, use instructions, installation assistance, spare parts availability, and so on.[3] The package of which he speaks is not the shipping container, but what is seen by the prospective buyer, and its principal purpose is to catch the eye of possible customers. This leads into the cultural or environmental aspects, wherein size, color, and design must take into consideration esthetics, income, and law (for example, requirements concerning marking). Companion to this primacy of the core product and its container is the element of instructions and literature, which may vary by market, language, and the need for and availability of repair facilities.

Analyzing a product from the viewpoint of making it optimally attractive to foreign markets has its limitations. Export may be so small a proportion of production that export management may not be able to influence product development or product policies, at least in the early years of the effort, when volume is very low. It may be hard enough to get even a part of production for export, especially if domestic demands ever become strong. Furthermore, from the viewpoint of effective distribution, it is usual to think in terms of a product line or lines. Sometimes one of the product lines of a diversified company may not employ the same distribution channels as another; moreover, at times it is advisable to be able to offer a full line. For example, a full line might be needed to facilitate or carry distribution overhead. In such instances it might be advantageous to add another company's production to one's own to round out the line offered.

Now we have seen that it is on the basis of product line, indicated volumes in each foreign market, and resource availability that a company is able to plan its production and distribution system, its financial and manpower requirements, the best organization for exporting, and so on. These are not independent; they influence each other and depend on each other.

Influence of the Product

A strong, if not determining, influence on the type of organization adopted to have a product reach international markets is the nature of the product itself. This goes for both the domestic unit and the form of distribution employed overseas. How-

---

[3] Franklin R. Root, *Strategic Planning for Export Marketing* (Scranton, Pennsylvania: International Textbook Company, 1966), p. 37.

ever, there is no hard-and-fast rule stating that only this or that form of organization is acceptable either domestically or abroad. Aside from the nature of the product, organization for exporting is also influenced most practically by individual situations within a company or country, and by volume—actual or potential. This is why we see one company using one channel of distribution for its export operation while its competition uses another, and why we see a company using one distributive channel in one country, and a different one in another.

Significance of Company Situation

Undertaking export activity involves a major risk and investment of time for many firms. One would be well advised, therefore, to undertake it only if understanding is gained at the outset as to what various levels of export activity mean in terms of both profit and resource requirements. Important in determining the availability of resources for commitment to overseas business is the extent of current domestic plans, which would also lay a claim to available resources. What domestic programs is a company currently planning or considering? What demand will these programs make on available resources, at what time, and for how long? Finally, what are the risks, possible returns, and timing of the programs?

Now let us take another and final view of the product implications:

1. The product must be something a foreign market wants; it must satisfy a known or an anticipated demand. If it can do this without modification, all well and good; if it is to be modified, there are additional problems.

2. There will likely be, or have to be, more than one product or model.

3. The type of product will determine, or at least influence, the best way to reach the foreign market. For example, if a product has a low value and necessitates repetitious purchases, one avenue can best be used. If it is technical or unique in matters of, say, health, it may call for licensing the manufacture abroad. If it is expensive, with one-time or infrequent sales, still another avenue can best be used. If it is complex and requires special training or servicing and a supply of parts, still another problem arises.

In summary, the product and the company situation are predetermined factors that are part of an existent, and presumably viable, business undertaking. We may try to isolate considerations of one or the other in regard to adaptation to foreign demand or the impact of entry into foreign markets, but they cannot really be separated. Positions have already been taken concerning each. The company is already making its product, so the product or product line has been selected; and the company has been established and financed for operating at a given level in the domestic market, so the selection and investment of resources will already have been made. To spill over internationally probably will involve pressures and modifications. Hence, company and product considerations play a most important role in the beginning or expansion of an export effort.

3

Distribution Channels

There is anything but uniformity in the structure of the distribution channels found in international trade. Here we are considering a function that can be performed by any of several people, in any of several ways. Kramer divides the international distribution system into two groups: international marketing channels in the home market and international marketing channels abroad. He states, "The distinction is made on the basis of the *location* of each particular channel, not on the *nationality* of those traders utilizing it."[1]

Many other writers and observers draw their broadest classification of distribution channels according to whether there is contact with the foreign importer or buyer (commonly referred to as *direct* or *indirect* exporting).

In either case, the job is the same: to get goods from here to there, from seller to buyer, and to keep them rolling:

- On time.
- In good condition.
- At an agreed-upon, mutually satisfactory price.
- With the seller being paid in accordance with the agreed-upon credit or financing arrangement.
- With the seller retaining control over the title and bearing responsibility for physical protection of the goods while en route, or at least until title passes to the buyer and risk of loss is assumed by him.
- In a quantity that will benefit both seller and buyer.
- With the continuing profitability of the operation.

Before looking into factors that would suggest the selection of one type of distribution channel over another for a particular product and in a particular country, it will be helpful to identify and classify typical channels that are widely accepted in business.

SALES IN THE UNITED STATES (INDIRECT EXPORTING)

For ease of reference, the first major category, sales made within the United States, is frequently referred to as indirect exporting because the manufacturer or merchant is not in direct touch with the foreign market. This does not mean, however, that the American producer deals with less specific markets or that American buyers are less demanding than purchasers in foreign countries. Indirect exporting channels are able to function only if they successfully fill the role of instructed or well-informed middlemen. Of primary significance to a manufacturer or other producer disposing of his output through indirect channels is that what the

---

[1] Roland L. Kramer, *International Marketing*, 3rd ed. (Cincinnati: Southwestern Publishing Company, 1970), p. 423.

purchasers do with what they buy and how it is traded abroad is no concern of his; he may never know to whom they sell abroad, and if sales are in protected or franchised territories of agents in other countries some friction may be anticipated.

In the other group of distribution channels, the exporter, say a manufacturer, is in direct touch with the foreign market. The following details and observations concerning each channel will suggest points that may indicate the advisability, if not the necessity, of employing one or the other in moving a company's production to a foreign market.

Foreign Buying Representatives (Resident Foreign Buyers)

Important in this group are purchases in the United States by resident foreign buyers, for foreign mines, oil companies, utilities, transportation companies, and so on. The principals may be of U.S., foreign, or joint ownership, and they represent a market for a wide range of products, such as oil-field equipment, mining machinery, and industrial and transportation equipment. Buying representatives include those purchasing for principals such as the Asiatic Petroleum Corporation, Chilean Nitrate Sales Corporation, Esso International Inc., and the National Railways of Colombia. Others, such as the Italian Federation of Farmers' Cooperatives in Washington and New York, are interested in the procurement of feed grain, livestock, farm machinery, pesticides, and other farm supplies.

Foreign Government Purchasing Missions

This channel sometimes represents the only or best way for sales to certain foreign markets to be accomplished. For example, countries receiving assistance from the U.S. Agency for International Development (AID) are obligated to purchase many items with such funds only from U.S. sources. These purchases can be controlled by and channeled through foreign government purchases. Other purchases by foreign governments, either voluntary or "tied" to U.S. sources, are those of military supply purchasing missions and other government purchasing offices. Typical of these are the India Supply Mission, in Washington; the French Tobacco Commissioner for the United States, in Baltimore; the Mexican Government Railway System, in New York; the head of trade and development, Nigerian Consulate General, New York; and the offices of commercial attachés of certain countries, usually in New York.

Another subgroup in this category is the centralized state-trading corporations. Probably the best known of these is the Amtorg Trading Corporation, which acts as agent for most of the foreign trade organizations in the USSR, and through which sales to Soviet buyers are arranged. In 1969 Poland was reported to be conducting its foreign trade through 43 foreign trade organizations, each chartered by the Ministry of Foreign Trade. Thirty-four of these are authorized to deal in designated commodities, and commercial representation abroad is through offices of trade counselors, commercial attachés attached to Polish diplomatic missions, and special trade missions.[2] Yugoslavia's foreign trade is not conducted through government purchasing agencies. Instead, it is carried on mainly by some 1,000 enterprises that are specially licensed to engage in foreign trade.[3] These foreign trade corporations are nominally independent but they must operate only within the framework of their country's overall foreign trade plan. In many countries besides these, foreign trade in one or several products is centralized under government operation.

Foreign Trading Companies

American offices of large international trading houses, such as the well-known Japanese firms Mitsui, Mitsubishi, Marubeni-Iida, and Sumitomo, often act as buying agents for their associates at home as well as purchasing for their own export sales abroad.

An important fact about this distribution channel is that through financial and family influences, the trading company may be expected to handle some competing production, hence to have to divide its attention. On the other hand, these same financial and family relationships may dictate that the only way to reach a certain segment of the market is through such trading firms; and the market is, in some cases, substantial. Furthermore, the worldwide connections of such firms in several countries can offer quick access to several foreign markets.

In some cases foreign owned outlets in the United States may

---

[2] U.S. Department of Commerce, "Basic Data on the Economy of Poland," *Overseas Business Reports, 69–39,* June 1969, pp. 14–15.

[3] U.S. Department of Commerce, "Selling in Yugoslavia," *Overseas Business Reports, 70–32,* July 1970, p. 1.

be incorporated there and therefore be American citizens, legally. So they could be seen as belonging in the category of American middlemen located in the United States. On the other hand, there are a number of primarily American firms or individuals whose job it is to buy in the United States (or Canada) for account of foreign principals or to buy on their own account and to export. These include such operations as export commission houses and export merchants.

Export Commission Houses

These experts in specific lines receive orders from foreign buyers and search out the most advantageous sources of supply. In effect, they act as purchasing agents and attend to the details of exporting. Obviously, they may also keep their eyes open for good opportunities to be suggested to their principals abroad. In any event, the key point is that they work on behalf of a foreign buyer, not the American producer, and are paid a commission by the foreign firm.

The importance of export commission houses appears to have declined in recent years, as communication and transportation facilities have improved, as markets have expanded, and as manufacturers have gone more into direct exporting. Although some firms still designate themselves export commission houses, many are composite organizations performing the functions of export commission houses and several other types of export business. For example, in its booklet *Directory of New York Buyers for Export,* the Canadian Consulate General in New York identifies several companies that are engaged in one or more of the functions of export agent, export merchant, and commission house.

Similar to the commission house is the export brokerage, commonly encountered in the food business and in the distribution of certain primary commodities. The brokers act merely as middlemen, without taking title to the goods going abroad. It is obvious that both avenues are appropriate for only a few products, such as those sold by some standard or classification (such as agricultural products or lumber or metals), or produced by small manufacturers not themselves in a position to export. They could not be well used for unique or differentiated products that are good candidates for aggressive market development or for manufactured specialties when consistent export markets are sought and relied on by producers.

Export Merchants and Trading Houses

By definition, a merchant buys and sells on his own account and runs the market risks. He must know his business and his products and, in order to have a large repeat business, which is essential to the continuous functioning of a distribution system, he must be able to depend on his source of supply and know that his channels abroad are open and friendly. Export merchants may handle a wide variety of products and some are known to handle anything. Although often referred to as export merchants, many of the better houses are active in both exports and imports and some are classed as trading companies.

A prime characteristic of these channels is that the producer usually does not know to whom the export merchants and trading houses sell abroad. Furthermore, they do not work primarily in his behalf, although it is to their interest to have dependable sources of supply. Among the larger and older companies, some of which have been in business for 50 or even 100 years, are W. R. Grace & Company; Dodge & Seymour, Ltd.; and Wessel Duval & Co., Inc. Most are located in New York.

Because some export channels buy on instruction of, and for account of, others, and because merchants and trading houses buy and sell on their own account, it must be expected that they may switch merchandise sources when advantageous. Therefore, a manufacturer might find that the use of export merchants or middlemen as a channel for moving his goods abroad results in a less dependable market; moreover, because there is no direct contact with foreign markets, there is little opportunity for obtaining market reaction or feedback.

SALES ABROAD (DIRECT EXPORTING)

The second major category of export distribution channels is sales abroad (direct exporting), in which the American producer is in direct touch with representatives or markets in other countries. Here we have two principal subgroups: independent businessmen abroad and home-office controlled outlets in foreign countries. As will be seen later, sometimes a producer retains some control over foreign distribution through contractual arrangements even though the foreign entity is an independent business or businessman. The main kinds of direct exporting follow.

Merchants (Wholesale and Retail)

A very significant channel, already established and operating in almost every country, is merchants, both wholesale and retail. They have their own distribution networks within the foreign country, including warehouses and a staff of salesmen, and they may be in a position to offer service, credit, and the like to prospective consumers abroad. It must be expected, however, that because they buy and sell at their own risk and work in their own interest, they will constantly be alert to opportunities to buy where it will be to their benefit. In some countries, an import house will sell at either wholesale or retail; in others, only at wholesale. Large retailers are very important direct outlets abroad, and stores like Harrod's or Liberty's of London, and Galeries Lafayette or Au Printemps, in Paris, or Takashimaya, in Tokyo, are in a position to absorb a significant part of the exports of many individual producers.

Another direct outlet abroad is the broker who specializes in staple commodities such as grain or metals and whose outlets are institutional, hard-nosed buyers. The latter purchase in large lots and function in a field less susceptible to advertising and sales or other promotional campaigns than do buyers of consumer goods or of manufactured products incorporating a high degree of technology.

Agents and Distributors

Agents and distributors represent the ultimate in direct foreign marketing through independent businessmen abroad. These two identifications are sometimes used interchangeably and may appear to overlap to some extent, but there is a distinction. An agent generally sells to an entire country, normally carries no inventory (at least for his own account), and sells to distributors, each of which may be franchised for subterritories of the agent's. As the manufacturing exporter's direct representative, he is paid a commission by him. An agent finds and keeps distributors satisfied, participates in advertising and other promotion, and may assist in clearing away problems such as licenses or customs formalities. Sales to distributors are commonly on credit, and usually such orders require the exporter's approval, although the agent may guarantee the credit to his principal. In this case, the account is sometimes referred to as a *del credere* arrangement, and the agent as a *del credere* agent.

On the other hand, a distributor buys and carries inventory and parts, and does servicing. He resembles and yet differs somewhat from a wholesaler in the standard sense, because he is frequently franchised for a defined territory and he is rather specialized as to product line. Distributors are often referred to as dealers, and, like agents, they participate in advertising.

In certain countries, such as Ceylon, Kuwait, Libya, and Iraq, only nationals are designated as agents, and these are the only persons authorized to import. Even when firms are established in some of these countries for the purpose of engaging in foreign trade, it may be required that the directors, if not all the stockholders, be nationals of that particular country.

Home-Office Controlled Representation

The foregoing designations pertain principally to independent businesses or businessmen abroad. But a large volume of exporting is conducted via home-office controlled representation, which in some cases permits more aggressive market development.

Acknowledging the fact that some exports may be accomplished by mail order, which must be called home-office controlled and must be considered direct exporting, we can say that the two principal outlets under home-office control are resident or traveling export salesmen and permanent establishments in the foreign markets. Export salesmen stationed abroad are most appropriate for the foreign sales of large unit-value items, when technical explanations or adaptability are advisable. Such sales include engineering and utilities installations, transportation facilities, and the like.

Sales subsidiaries and other permanent establishments abroad (mainly manufacturing or assembly facilities) are a very important avenue for reaching foreign markets directly. It is estimated that a little over half of the 1965 exports of 320 U.S. parent firms with foreign affiliates were consigned to these affiliates.[4] Some affiliates are for sales only, and some involve assembly and/or manufacturing as well as sales. Maintenance of a permanent establishment in another country, whether for sales only or for other operations as well, gives rise to the consideration of taxation. This can be a deciding factor in determining whether a home-controlled distribution channel should be established abroad and, if so, what type it will be.

---

[4] U.S. Department of Commerce, "U.S. Exports to Foreign Affiliates of U.S. Firms," *Survey of Current Business,* May 1969, p. 34.

The channels an exporter uses are influenced, if not practically determined, by some factors that are within his control and by others that are not. However, as we have seen, the main choice, assuming he has the resources to make a choice, is between *indirect* exporting, wherein the producer sells to someone else who does the exporting, and *direct* exporting, wherein the producer himself is the actual exporter who is in direct touch with buyers or representatives overseas.

The following lists summarize some of the principal implications of employing direct rather than indirect channels of exporting. The responsibilities, obligations, and benefits may or may not be bearable or sought by an exporter, but they are the features that must at some time be considered in relation to the company's product, structure, and financial and manpower position.

The objectives and benefits listed are available through direct exporting, and the indicated responsibilities or obligations fall on a company to the extent that it uses direct channels to move its goods abroad.

These objectives and benefits are:

- Some degree of control over distribution, specifically: selling price, sales area, protection of franchised territories of agents and distributors.
- Assurance that one's product will not be neglected for a competing line.
- Opportunity for more feedback from foreign markets, with resultant enhanced opportunity to effect modifications or adaptations of the product to satisfy market demand.
- Increased opportunity for protection of trademark and for building up goodwill.
- Aggressive development of individual foreign markets.
- Full return on sales abroad; no sharing of profits.

The operational or functional responsibilities are:

- Maintenance of adequate current commercial intelligence on several foreign markets.
- Detailed analysis of each selected foreign market.
- Selection of distribution channels and of representatives in each of several foreign markets.
- Establishment of goals, quotas, or targets for each market.
- Decision as to export pricing.
- Credit investigation of buyers.

- Modification or redesign of products for foreign buyers.
- Advertising and other sales promotion effort abroad.
- Servicing and maintenance, if needed, including technical training and installation. May have to be direct from factory at times.
- Mastery of technical details pertaining to documents, to U.S. and foreign trade regulations, to transportation rates and shipping schedules, to financing techniques, to translations, and so on.

The financial obligations are:

- Risks of credit collections and of refusal to accept merchandise on arrival.
- Carrying of accounts receivable due from foreigners.
- Carrying of larger and possibly more varied inventory; possibly maintenance of or assistance in carrying inventories overseas for quick deliveries.
- Adequate resources to support added costs pertaining to selling expenses, development and training of export organization, modifications or adaptations in production, transportation and insurance under c.i.f. (cost, insurance, and freight) quotations.
- Larger initial outlay before profits are shown.

4

Organization for Exporting

Within a company, the system adopted for carrying on its export activity is influenced primarily by the company's size and financial condition, product(s), intent and degree of involvement in exports, and export volume. Types of organization for export may vary from almost casual to formal and legal differentiation.

ORGANIZATIONAL ARRANGEMENTS

Built-in Export Function

The simplest arrangement is that commonly referred to as a built-in function, wherein export responsibility is simply appended to the domestic activities of the existing departments or divisions. In effect, the export manager or salesman simply draws on the company's packing, shipping, insurance, advertising, and treasury departments, and so on, for taking care of the several specialized tasks that must be performed for exports, including that of documentation. However, such an arrangement is viable only for companies with small-scale or limited interest in exports, and it can be handled by one man and a secretary. But sooner or later, as expansion occurs, such a limited structure cannot endure. Transportation and financial problems arise, translations have to be done, foreign market demands or peculiarities become apparent, pricing and relations with foreign distributors become more significant, foreign travel becomes advisable or necessary, advertising and market development call for attention, and stress and strain between loyalty to domestic and foreign operations appear.

Separate Export Department

The logical step is to break away to some extent and move to a separate export department, where some of the routine and specialized functional jobs are taken over from other servicing departments interested primarily in domestic operations and are set up to concentrate on exports. Eventually this kind of department may evolve into an international division and even into one or more separate export sales corporations.

Separate Export Corporations

Tax considerations may also become a problem of some significance, and separate domestic export sales corporations may be called for. One of the important stimuli to this type of organization is the income tax saving of 14 percentage points on income earned by Western Hemisphere Trade Corporations. To qualify for this benefit, the corporation, which must be chartered in the United States, must meet three specifications: all business, except incidental purchases, must be done in the Western Hemisphere; 90 percent of its gross income must be from the active conduct of a trade or business; and 95 percent of its gross income must be derived from sources outside the United States.

Further moves in the area of taxes may be anticipated if a proposal introduced in 1970 is enacted into law by Congress. It would provide for the deferral of United States income tax for a domestic corporation engaged in export sales. Such corporations would be known as Domestic International Sales Corporations (DISC). Legislation authorizing this organizational arrangement had not been passed by late 1971, but the proposal had strong administration support and drew substantial business backing.[1] Among the business groups endorsing the concept were the National Association of Manufacturers, the Machinery and Allied Products Institute, and the Council of State Chambers of Commerce. It was opposed by the AFL–CIO and others.

Proponents of the idea felt that existing U.S. tax treatment of foreign source income involves a bias in favor of large corporations and that the deferral proposed, similar to that provided for foreign manufacturing subsidiaries of U.S. companies, would provide smaller corporations with equal opportunity for tax deferral on foreign source income arising from export sales. The U.S. tax on export income derived through DISC would be deferred as long as it is either used in the corporation's export business, invested in defined export-related assets of the DISC, or invested in Eximbank paper (obligations issued to it) and thus is not distributed to the DISC's shareholders.

In order to qualify as a DISC, two principal requirements would have to be met. First, 95 percent of the DISC's income would have to be derived from export sales activities, from investments in export-related assets, and/or from Eximbank paper. Second, 95 percent of the DISC's assets would have to be used in its export business or be in the form of export-related assets or Eximbank paper. A DISC would be required to confine its activities almost entirely to export selling and certain related activities, and it could sell the products of any domestic producer to any foreign purchaser, whether or not related, for a foreign destination. Thus a DISC could operate through its own foreign sales subsidiaries.

The foregoing organizational arrangements are all within the company, so to speak, either on the basis of salaried officers and employees or through parent company ownership of a subsidiary chartered in the United States. There are, in addition, some organi-

[1] U.S. Department of Commerce, "DISC Proposal Is Detailed," *International Commerce*, May 25, 1970, pp. 18–21.

zational arrangements that rest on the use of independent export management under contract and on cooperative undertakings in export.

Combination Export Managers

Chief among the independent export managers are businessmen who handle exports for a commission paid by the seller. A manufacturers' export agent is a foreign trade specialist who, when handling a number of products or lines, as is common practice, is known as a combination export manager (CEM). These lines are, or should be, allied and noncompetitive. A combination export manager acts as the export department for each of the manufacturers whose products he handles. The CEM is independent in the sense that he stands between the manufacturer and foreign customers and is not a regular, full-time member of the manufacturer's organization. Depending on arrangements between him and the manufacturer, the CEM may and often does carry on foreign correspondence on the manufacturer's letterhead and, in effect, he is the manufacturer's export manager.

Combination export managers offer genuine advantages, especially to manufacturers who are just beginning to turn to export markets or who wish to try new foreign markets for the first time. The expertise they immediately provide is a distinct asset in the early stages of exporting, and they facilitate a manufacturer's access to one or more foreign markets without a large commitment of funds other than those needed for added inventory and possibly for receivables. Many arrangements wherein manufacturers channel their foreign sales through CEMs are of several years' standing, and cases have been reported in which a manufacturer, after breaking away from his CEM and trying to do the business himself, came back to the CEM because of the comparative costs and efficiency.

Depending on its size and the number and types of accounts handled, a CEM company may be organized into departments. For example, one of the larger and better-known CEM firms, Ballagh and Thrall, Inc., of Philadelphia, acts as export manager for over 40 manufacturers whose products vary among automotive, electrical, and fire-fighting equipment, instruments, industrial products, plastics and machinery, pumps, office equipment, and consumer goods. Some 5,000 U.S. manufacturers are estimated to reach foreign markets through CEMs, which are said to handle at least 10 percent of the finished and semifinished manufactured goods exported from the United States.[2]

A key feature of working through a CEM is that the CEM's primary allegiance is to the manufacturer, who pays his commission and makes the distribution arrangement with him. This arrangement covers such points as products to be handled, territory, price, and conditions of sale. In this respect it is similar to working directly with an agent located in a foreign country, but naturally the area involved with the CEM is much broader, because he normally has worldwide export representation for his manufacturers. A CEM does everything for a manufacturer that a salaried export manager would do, but he does it for a commission. He appoints agents abroad for the manufacturer, educates them, starts quotations and price negotiations back and forth, follows up on delivery, obtains necessary export licenses, provides translation services, makes up documents, arranges insurance, banks documents, and in some cases may also manage credit.

Although CEMs are of primary interest to manufacturers, the names of 27 were listed in *Foreign Agriculture* a few years ago as handling U.S. foods and produce. In reviewing the services that CEMs offer to smaller producers of food products, the article stated that a CEM might "export one processor's canned applesauce, apple slices, and apple juice; another's canned peaches and pears; and another's canned vegetables. Such a setup allows him not only to make large shipments but also to sell several lines to a single customer and to spread promotion and research expenses." [3]

There is nothing that limits a manufacturer's export agent to operating solely as a CEM. It may, depending on its client's wishes and needs, buy a client's production outright and sell at its own risk. In this case the CEM company functions as a trader or merchant rather than as an export agent. In other words, a firm may be operating in more than one capacity.

Cooperative Exporting

Many manufacturers simply have too small a volume of potential exports to warrant the establishment of an in-house export department. In this case, larger firms already in international market-

---

[2] Dun and Bradstreet, "Combination Export Managers," *Business Abroad*, March 4, 1968, p. 17.

[3] U.S. Department of Agriculture, *Foreign Agriculture*, June 27, 1966, p. 10.

ing find it advantageous to take on the foreign distribution of allied products both to help in distributing their own and because it is profitable. Hence the idea of cooperative exporting, whereby big companies export the products of smaller ones that have no overseas distribution of their own. This is sometimes called "piggy-back" or "mother-hen" exporting.

Cooperative exporting received a strong boost from the Department of Commerce in the 1960s as a means of encouraging more producers to look to export markets to improve the U.S. balance of payments position. It is reported that some large companies have engaged in this practice for many years. For example, Armco Steel Corporation was reported as exporting the metal doors and frames made by Steelcraft Manufacturing Company of Cincinnati; the Pillsbury Company, the jams and jellies made by the J. M. Smucker Company; and Borg-Warner Corporation, the Toastmaster® products made by McGraw-Edison. Arrangements for acquiring and handling such exports vary from outright purchase (in which case it is similar to selling to or through an export merchant) to the use of promotional literature, to buying from the producer on the basis of orders generated.

Finally, a little-used but legally permitted domestic organization for export is a joint arrangement by exporters of similar products. This arrangement, permitted by the Webb-Pomerene Act of 1918, offers relief from application of the Sherman Act of 1890 provided that the firms are in the association for the sole purpose of engaging in export trade and are actually engaged in such export trade. However, for the exception to hold, an association's actions must not be in restraint of trade within the United States, nor in restraint of the export trade of any domestic competitor of such association. The association can do nothing to artificially or intentionally enhance or depress prices of the same class of goods in the United States, or to substantially lessen or otherwise restrain trade in the United States.

The Webb-Pomerene Act provides that the prohibition against unfair methods of competition in the Federal Trade Commission Act extend to unfair methods of competition in export trade, even though the acts constituting such unfair methods are done outside the territorial jurisdiction of the United States. Surveillance of the Act is the responsibility of the Federal Trade Commission, with which Webb-Pomerene associations must register and file annual reports.

A Webb-Pomerene association may act as export sales agent for its members; promote conferences and agreements in export trade; develop its members' products abroad; agree upon prices, terms, and sales policies in export trade; allocate export business among its members; arrange for insurance, freight rates, and cargo space; and collect and disseminate trade information concerning foreign markets.[4] These associations have never been important in U.S. export trade. Since 1918 a total of about 230 associations have been formed, representing some 4,000 member exporters. Many of these did not last long, and the number existing in early 1971 was 34. Nor have they been significant in overall trade; the value of exports attributable to them in recent years is in the neighborhood of 4 to 5 percent of the U.S. total.

Joint Export Associations (JEA)

Still another type of cooperative exporting was introduced in early 1969 when the Department of Commerce announced the signing of contracts with the first five industry groups under a new joint government-business program to expand exports. Under the program the Commerce Department would contract with trade associations or groups of firms for the systematic development of specific export markets for particular products over a sustained period. The government and the joint export association would share costs such as market research, advertising, publicity, supplying samples and technical data, participating in trade exhibitions, overseas promotion visits, and training sales and service personnel.

The five contracts represented participation by 78 companies from 15 states. The contractors were four combination export management firms and a trade consortium. In August 1970, three additional contracts were signed with representatives of 39 companies in 15 states. As of late 1971, however, further expansion of the program appeared in doubt, since an announcement was made that because of cuts in the budget for export promotion, the program would be phased out and no further JEA's would be approved at that time.

SELECTION OF DISTRIBUTION CHANNELS

Several channels of distribution can be utilized to have one's production reach foreign markets, and several types of domestic or-

---

[4] Walter S. Surrey and Crawford Shaw, *A Lawyer's Guide to International Business Transactions* (Philadelphia: Joint Committee on Continuing Legal Education, 1963), p. 636.

ganization can be employed or adopted to carry on export activities. One distribution channel can be used for several markets, different channels can be used for the same product in different markets, and different channels can be used for different products in the same market.

There are several key factors in the selection of distribution channels to be utilized in international trade, and sometimes any single one will be of overriding importance in a given situation. These include, as a minimum, type of product, financial situations of seller and buyer, the ease or difficulty of selling in each foreign market, volume expected, intent of the manufacturer, customs of the trade, and laws and regulations of the countries involved. All are important and no one is always supreme.

Type of Product

Is it crude, semimanufactured, or manufactured?
Is it capital goods or consumer goods?
  If the latter, is it soft or durable?
Is it easy or hard to sell?
  What is the nature of the end-user? Can he be influenced? For example, can an exporter's man get into a factory and talk to the men on the job who use the product or whose technical views would influence purchase?
Is there a factor of seasonality in production or consumption?
Is the product of high or of low unit-value?
What is the pattern of sales (frequency and size)?
Is servicing or after-sales attention needed?
Is a supply of spare parts needed; and is repair easy or complicated, requiring special training or tools?
Is advertising necessary or advisable, or even permitted?

Merely reviewing such a list of characteristics suggests that certain types of organizations are almost dictated by these considerations.

Financial Situations of Seller and Buyer

In foreign trade a number of factors suggest that more funds are needed for export business than for domestic. For example, longer transportation time is commonly involved; the supplying of larger, if not vastly different, markets imposes the need for carrying larger inventories, which in turn require additional funds; and longer credit terms mean the carrying of more receivables, or additional financial arrangements that relieve the seller from or assist him in carrying receivables needed to meet other suppliers' competitive credit terms.

Moreover, though a buyer abroad may be able and willing to make payment, he may be impeded from doing so by his government. The result is likely to be slow collection and a larger volume of receivables. This means that more financial resources are needed. Even if these differences did not exist, even if trading conditions were the same for foreign as for domestic activities, the financial standing of both the foreign distributors and the domestic producer influences the choice of channels used. One may simply not be able to carry his full weight, so the other must help. For example, buyers often finance suppliers or sign long-term contracts that aid them in financing.

Ease or Difficulty of Selling Abroad

Assuming, now, that the decision to enter a foreign market means that the market is to be aggressively developed and not just casually supplied, one is faced with the need to know the market in detail. Gaining detailed knowledge of many foreign markets may be difficult if a company is spread too thin to know them all well; instead, a concentration on one or a few might be more in order. Perhaps different organization could be used for different markets. Obviously it would take a very large staff of marketing experts to analyze and follow developments in a number of markets (assuming the company is in a position to supply the market potential). Furthermore, usually foreigners or specialists know more about their own markets than we do. Therefore, one must question the wisdom of competing with the established professionals. We may find that the best answer is to use them; it may be less expensive, give quicker results, and be less troublesome administratively.

Volume Expected

Every organization or organizational unit can pay its way only when sales volume is adequate to cover all costs. But there are certain basic, minimal costs that have to be anticipated even with small volume. If anticipated volume is not sufficient to pay for specialists, then the type of distribution organization is somewhat predetermined. Expertise comes with specialization and repetition, and in many cases expertise is needed. Hence, the question is whether one will try to be his own expert or whether he will use others. That, too, dictates somewhat the distribution channel and type of organization to be employed.

Intent of the Manufacturer

In foreign trade, some exporters are interested only in selling through an intermediary; some are interested in going in on a big scale—in *direct* contact with the foreign market and in rather aggressive development of it. If the latter is the intent of the manufacturer, he must consider the expense of setting up an export department, with all of its ramifications and specialization as business grows, and the expense of selecting agents abroad and working with them, contributing to their effort, and encouraging them in a sort of joint venture undertaking.

Customs of the Trade

Depending on the country and even the region within a country, one finds differing acceptances of what can be called formal or typical levels of distribution. In some cases there will be clear wholesale and retail channels; in some, it is practically, if not legally, impossible to cross over; in others, there is considerable crossing over, with the same firm abroad acting as either wholesaler or retailer. This must be taken into account, and one must recognize the implications of volume and "normal" trading arrangements.

In addition, some retailers are larger in size and in potential import volume than are some wholesalers, so again an exporter will be faced with weighing a concentration on one larger retailer (or retail-wholesaler) or on a smaller wholesaler who may be looking for several retail outlets.

Laws of Foreign Countries

Commercial conditions in foreign markets play a very important part in determining the distribution channel and form of organization to be adopted; in fact, they may practically dictate it. For example, an exporter may consider establishing his own sales office or subsidiary in a foreign country. But he finds, as in the case of Kuwait, Ceylon, Iraq, and Libya, that by the law of these countries, import trade is restricted to nationals. Only they can be officially registered as agents or permitted to obtain import licenses, so there is no choice but to appoint one of them as agent or distributor.

The kind of distribution channel used to sell to a government or a state-trading agency is not the same as that used to sell to a network of distributors through an agent. Consider the tobacco monopolies in France or Italy, or the French coal-buying arrangement, Association Technique de l'Importation Charbonnière. Here, an exporter needs no inventory and usually not more than one man. Credit arrangements, if any, possibly are different from those used in sales to a number of distributors. In this case there would be one big sale, or a few, to a monopoly. Of course, the monopoly position enables the buyer to play one seller against another more effectively, and he may not work in any single exporter's interest, but there is no choice; it is the way things are done.

The same considerations apply to doing business with centralized state-trading establishments. Take the case of countries like Rumania, Czechoslovakia, Poland, Yugoslavia, Communist China, and the USSR. Not only is their trade handled by assigned monopolies; some may have buying (and selling) offices in the United States. The structures and practices of these are described in occasional issues of the U.S. Department of Commerce's *Overseas Business Reports* in the series titled "Foreign Trade Regulations of ——," and in other publications such as Canada's *Foreign Trade.*

Influence of Large Foreign Trading Companies

Apart from state trading, there is another very interesting area —Japan. The foreign trade market of Japan is characterized by giant trading companies, which are said to do about 75 percent of total Japanese trade.[5] The 12 biggest firms handle over 50 percent of all Japanese exports and about 60 percent of total imports. In fact, some experts say that practically no firms, except petroleum companies, import on their own account. So one may be almost forced to go through one of these giants. Smaller importers in Japan may not be able to give national distribution, and may have trouble selling to buyers tied to the trading groups. On the other hand, the trading groups include producers and therefore may not be the best outlet for an American exporter's goods, especially if they compete with those of their own affiliates.

---

[5] *Business Week,* January 8, 1966, p. 76.

5

Technical and Procedural Aspects: Financial

Many detailed steps must be taken on the way from the initial quotation by a seller to the receipt of goods and payment by the buyer. Some must be taken in a particular sequence. For example, before an offer can be made or an order received, a price must be established and the point of transfer of the goods specified. Transportation and all accumulated costs up to this point are included in the price. This is the first technical function to be performed in exporting.

Assuming now that an order has been received and accepted

and that all conditions of sale have been agreed upon, the following steps, which are not all-inclusive and not necessarily sequential, indicate the procedures involved in an export shipment using ocean transportation.

1. An export license must be obtained if required. With two exceptions (exports from the continental United States to its territories and possessions, and most exports to Canada for internal consumption) commercial exports from the United States and its territories or possessions are prohibited unless the Department of Commerce has either issued a validated license or established a general license permitting such shipments. For certain products, licenses may be required from other government agencies. (See Chapter 6.)

2. Export packing must be done either by the exporter himself or by a professional packer. Proper packing and marking must take into consideration the regulations of a number of authorities or interested participants in the international movement of cargo. Among these are inland carriers, ocean carriers, insurance companies, the Interstate Commerce Commission and the Coast Guard of the United States, and especially the regulations of the importing countries, some of which have prescribed standards that regulate the sizes of shipping containers.

3. Shipping space must be booked in advance in most cases, and alternatives in routing may offer important savings in time, transport costs, and safety. Cartage and delivery to wharf or inland carrier is necessary.

4. Necessary bills of lading (usually one for each type of carrier) must be prepared, and signed by the carriers.

5. Payment of wharfage or storage charges, or of transportation charges, may have to be made by an exporter and included in his price quotation, such as when quoting c.i.f. Also, some countries do not permit collect freight shipments. This restriction apparently is related to exchange controls.

6. Weighing and sampling by independent specialists must be arranged if required or requested.

7. Certificates of inspection must be obtained if required.

8. Shippers' export declarations must be prepared and filed with customs authorities, in some cases before shipment can be made.

9. Certificates of origin, properly authenticated, must be obtained if required or advisable. These have come into increasing interest in recent years in connection with duty rates applicable to preferential trading areas.

10. Commercial invoices must be prepared.

11. Consular invoices must be prepared and presented for certification as required by the country of destination.

12. Marine (air) insurance—policy or certificate—must be contracted for.

13. A draft on the foreign buyer or on a specified bank must be prepared and must have attached to it all prescribed documents for presentation to the bank for collection, payment, or acceptance.

In examining technical and procedural aspects, our interest is restricted to the more important ones. Only casual recognition need be given here to such specialty problems as marking, export packing, labeling, port charges, special transportation, or handling charges; the point is that each one entails costs that must be taken into account in pricing, no matter who pays them directly.

The most significant procedural considerations are those directly related to:

Pricing and price quotations.

Documents, many of which are unique to international trade and are designed to provide evidence or assurance that someone has done what he is supposed to do or that the merchandise is what or where it is supposed to be, in apparent good condition.

Coordination of the physical movement of goods with financial and transportation arrangements and in conformity with governmental requirements. This may be looked on as a complex logistical exercise.

PRICING AND PRICE QUOTATIONS

Sales volume is important in reaching and staying above the breakeven point in operations, and exporting is or may be important to individual businesses in reaching and maintaining a profit position. However, the breakeven concept cannot readily be used for the pricing of each product. Sometimes a low sales price on one product may generate sale of another, on which the gain is adequate to cover both. Moreover, prices cannot be set on cost plus established or hoped-for margin, at least not uniformly by product or country. In fact, price differentials between customers in the same country or between different countries are common. One could not for long sell at less than cost plus necessary margin, or opportunity income (income that could be earned by funds in places other than where now invested) would attract resources to alternative uses. However, certain factors do bring about pressure to quote lower prices abroad than in the United States. One is that the levels of income vary in different markets. Another is that lower prices may be quoted by domestic or by other foreign suppliers. Companion to this is the fact that if a given price is all that a market will bear, and it is lower than the United States price, it may still be in a company's interest to trade in the product because it may absorb part of the company's total overhead.

On the demand side, one must consider what the traffic will bear. When ball-point pens were novel it was difficult to find one at less than $14.50; today, 69¢ is not the lowest price. So in exporting it is necessary to hold prices down not only to take advantage of elastic demand, but also to discourage competition.

Our interest here is pricing and price quotation in export trade, so it is appropriate to recognize the main elements in export pricing. To do this, one must usually begin with the domestic price, which presumably covers all costs and yields a profit to the company. But in international trade one is competing in a foreign market, where the effective, competitive price must take into consideration all landed costs, with duty paid, no matter who directly pays it. What this means is that the closer an exporter gets to his customer abroad, the better (by quoting, say, c.i.f. foreign country instead of f.o.b. United States). A buyer wants to be able to calculate his total cost with as little trouble as possible. A seller, on the other hand, must ask whether his prices quoted abroad should be the same, higher, or lower than those quoted in the United States; he will quickly cast out the "same," simply because distribution costs differ between the two markets. This leaves the choice between higher or lower prices than in domestic business.

Prices Higher for Export

In some cases, prices quoted for export should be higher than when destined for the internal market because certain elements of cost related to sales abroad do not apply to domestic sales. Some of these are:

Advertising. Certainly the cost of advertising abroad—in foreign journals and through other media—is not a cost applicable to domestic sales.

Packing, marking, and labeling. Export packing, which is done to accommodate to risks peculiar to international transportation and in some cases to satisfy foreign government requirements, is an expense that does not apply to domestic markets. The same holds for marking and labeling conforming to foreign requirements.

Transportation. At least part of this physical, direct charge applies only to the merchandise moving out of the country and therefore is not called for in computing domestic costs f.o.b. factory. However, when quotations are made other than ex factory, c.i.f. for example, the cost of insurance and freight must be added to ex factory price and included in an export price quotation.

Foreign travel. Here, also, the cost is direct, an expense to exports and not to domestic business.

Other costs clearly attributable to exports and not to domestic sales include translations, special documentation, modification or adaptation for export markets, longer credit terms and collection periods, added political and economic risks (some of which are covered by insurance), salary and other costs related to the export manager and his staff, and direct selling expenses.

These considerations prompt the question of why one should sell abroad at all unless the price is higher. Why not sell more in the United States? Here one becomes involved in market segment considerations, interpretation of the nature of demand, domestic market potential outlook, and the like.

Prices Lower for Export

Just as certain costs create a need for higher prices, others suggest that some export prices be lower than domestic prices. This is simple recognition that certain elements in domestic pricing do not apply to international sales. For example, some of the expenses of domestic direct sales and advertising in no way apply to sales abroad. Also, some administrative costs that pertain primarily to domestic operations cannot be allocated to international pricing. Some shared administrative costs (indirect expenses) can properly be allocated, but here the problem is reaching a fair basis for allocation.

Certain taxes applicable to domestic sales, such as excises and sales taxes, may not apply to exports. This is a contentious problem between the United States and some European countries. The latter use a tax on value added at a rather high figure and rebate the tax on export sales. This rebate is permissible under GATT rules. The United States, relying more heavily on direct taxes (on income), cannot rebate the income tax on earnings from exports and is unable to offer what appear to be comparable rebates on competitive sales into third country markets. This argument can be overdone, however, because what it boils down to is that certain foreign countries rebate a tax that they impose on their own domestic markets but which the United States does not employ, so a 20 percent tax removed from a 20 percent tax is the same as zero removed from zero.

Another tax that may apply domestically but is lifted on exports is customs duty, which is rebated upon exportation by the process known as drawbacks.

In addition to the foregoing rather easily identifiable costs, other points must be considered when competing in a foreign market. One of these is foreign customs duties, which are paid by the importer and which may be an important segment of a buyer's total, final cost. Someone must, of course, pay all these costs. An exporter cannot ignore their impact, either on a delivered price or on a quotation f.o.b. some point in the United States. An exporter cannot ignore them, for the reason that competition may not ignore. Competition may, by adjusting prices downward, absorb part of the added costs that make themselves felt on the firing line—in the foreign marketplace. Here, however, one must be alert to the possibility of being accused of "dumping," that is, selling goods at prices lower than in the home (or sometimes other) markets, in which case an added duty may be imposed.

These and other cost elements have a bearing on a price quotation that must make an impact in a foreign market. Many of the cost elements may be indicated on a costing sheet, or export pricing sheet, which provides for at least recognition of some of these items. Failure to take the applicable ones into account when setting a c.i.f. price will result in a lower price than necessary to show a profit, or at least in a lower profit than desired. It will not result in a just price for the exporting company. On the other hand, excessive charges not actually required may mean loss of sales.

Ideally, one should begin with his own cost—ex factory, in the case of a producer; invoice, in the case of a merchant. The ex factory cost presumably covers applicable production and administrative and financial costs, not distribution costs applicable solely to domestic markets, or sales or excise taxes applicable only to domestic sales. The ex factory cost is frequently used as the basis for computing a percentage for profit, and as the figure on which an overseas representative's commission is based. The list of detailed costs that may come in for consideration is extensive.[1] At some

[1] J. R. Arnold illustrates this in "How to Work Out Export Prices," *Foreign Trade*, Department of Industry, Trade, and Commerce, Ottawa, Canada, May 15, 1965, p. 12; and "Use a Costing Sheet," *International Trade Forum*, International Trade Centre, *UNCTAD*/GATT, Geneva, February 1969, p. 18.

point other costs must also be recognized, such as export department costs (salaries, communications, and overhead) and advertising or sales promotion costs incurred in working with overseas representatives.

Intercompany Pricing

A substantial amount of American exports goes to subsidiaries or affiliates of American companies abroad. Here an exporting company faces selling to itself. Its intercompany pricing policy is a factor in determining how much of its taxable earnings is to be shown in each of the countries in which it is active.

Governments also have a direct interest in intercompany pricing, from three points of view. One is taxation, the second is dumping, and the third is cost in order to ascertain "national content," which determines a product's country of origin and its qualification for preferential treatment in the intratrade of regional arrangements such as free trade associations in which members may each impose different external tariffs but among which no tariff applies.

The pricing of transactions between an American corporation and its related companies is subject to challenge for tax purposes by the U.S. Treasury Department. Under authority of Section 482 of the Internal Revenue Act, U.S. tax officials may reallocate income between an American taxpaying corporation and its related companies, including its foreign affiliates, by determining that the price charged a foreign affiliate was too low or that the price paid a foreign affiliate was too high. Through such directed change and reallocation of resulting income between company units in the United States and in a foreign country, the tax base is affected. Other countries themselves are interested in seeing that they get a fair share of profits, which can then be taxed and brought into the foreign exchange earnings and use picture.

In applying cost and price considerations to international transactions between related companies, a few elementary distinctions are in order. The first is between direct costs, which must be taken into account in all pricing, and indirect, or joint costs, which involve shared expenses. The latter include elements such as administrative salaries (of the president and other top officers, who may be located in the United States), correspondence, legal and similar costs incurred in the United States in the total corporate interest, and departmental expenses whose functions are shared between domestic and international sales, such as those of the shipping and credit departments.

Effective allocation of costs can have two major objectives. One is to develop a more accurate measure of profitability and comparison for internal control purposes; the other is to reduce the total tax burden on a company. Some firms are reported to prefer not to allocate joint costs between domestic and international operations on a daily basis because they consider that doing so implies a value judgment. Moreover, it may result in a shifting of profits and thus weaken the validity of profits as a measure of comparative performance. A contribution to profit concept of sales is considered as possibly more meaningful, with absorption of overhead based on some acceptable broad formula such as the ratio of a subsidiary's sales or assets to the company's total. In addition, gains or losses as a result of foreign exchange fluctuations can be a significant factor in determining comparative export performances.

The profitability of a foreign subsidiary, which is its base for corporate income tax, can be influenced by company decisions as to charges to cover parent company or total corporate expenses. Because income tax rates are not the same in all countries a company may find it advantageous to make heavier charges (thus reducing taxable income) to its operations in countries with high income tax rates and to reduce its charges (thus increasing the subsidiary's taxable income) where the income tax rate is lighter.

Allocation must be accomplished through prices on goods sold to a related company abroad or through periodic charges to foreign operations, such as to foreign sales subsidiaries. These charges may take the form of service or technical fees or levies added to the basic cost of goods sold to the related company. This, however, is not as simple as it may sound because indirect expenses that are allocable in one country (taxing jurisdiction) may not be in another.

In addition to foreign laws relating to such charges, there is always the question of what the U.S. Internal Revenue Service will consider a reasonable charge or cost to a related person abroad. Other considerations are the policies of different host countries regarding remittance of profit, the availability of foreign exchange to cover services and fees, and the repatriation of capital. These will likely affect a company's decision about what its records show about where its profits are made. Finally, there is the element of company preference as to how costs are to be allocated for comparative or guideline purposes.

Currency Considerations in Pricing and Price Quotations

Quotations on an export or import inquiry or on an offer by the United States exporter may be denominated in U.S. dollars or in a foreign currency. Our customer (or supplier) is abroad and his type of money is not the one we use, and vice versa. Whose currency is to be used in making the quotation? Either we will get (or pay) a currency we do not use or the foreign businessman will pay (or receive) U.S. dollars, a currency he does not normally use. This means that we have to be concerned with foreign exchange.

First, let us recall why foreign exchange rates change, and think over what even a slight change means in business transactions. One reason for a change in rates is, obviously, *demand* for a particular currency in terms of dollars. This demand can have its roots in many factors, because all involve the purchase of another currency to cover transactions denominated in that currency or the sale of U.S. dollars received by the foreigner if he were paid in dollars. Some of the factors are:

Merchandise imports by the United States (but at time of settlement, not an aggregate for a full year).
Purchase of securities from foreigners (either U.S. or foreign securities; this does not include U.S. investments paid for in kind, as by the export of machinery).
Interest and dividend payments to foreigners.
U.S. tourist expenditures.
Private remittances to families, friends, or charities.
Services—transportation, advertising, insurance, and so on.
Capital movements (arising from interest rate differentials).
Purchases by Federal Reserve to maintain foreign exchange rates (or sale of dollars by foreign monetary authorities).
Adjustments in bank "positions" due to customer transactions.

The opposite factor, *supply*, is reflected in a demand for dollars by those with pounds, francs, marks, yen, and so on.

Suppose we examine a few recent rate changes and translate them into impact on individual companies. For this purpose, Table 6 is illustrative. The quotations were selected at random and pertain to the foreign exchange of the country shown in terms of U.S. dollars. The table shows that, had a sale been made by a U.S. exporter in April 1969, in terms of Canadian dollars and on three-month credit terms, the Canadian dollar would have been worth 0.427 percent less at the time payment fell due than it was when the price was set. This works out to an annual rate of decline in value of 1.71 percent. Had a sale been made anywhere in terms of French francs, in April 1969, on six-month credit terms, the francs received when payment fell due would have been worth 11.1 percent less than when contracted for. (The French franc was devalued effective August 10, 1969, from 4.94 to 5.55 francs per U.S. dollar.) This means, too, that had prices been quoted in U.S. dollars, the dollars would have cost the French debtor 11 percent more than when he made his purchase. On the opposite side of the coin, had a sale been made in terms of German marks in July 1969, on four-month credit terms, the marks received would have been worth 8.4 percent more than when the sale was made. (The German mark was revalued from 4.0 to 3.66 to the U.S. dollar effective October 26, 1969.)

Table 6. Selected foreign exchange rate changes in 1969–1970 (computed on basis of U.S. cents per foreign currency unit).

Country	*Date*	*Number of Months*	*Percent of Change*	*Annual Rate of Change (%)*
Australia	April '69–Sept. '69	5	−0.3865	−0.928
	Sept. '69–April '70	7	+0.9209	+1.578
Belgium	Sept. '69–March '70	6	+1.328	+2.656
Canada	April '69–July '69	3	−0.4273	−1.709
	Dec. '69–April '70	4	+0.1332	+0.400
Denmark	Dec. '69–April '70	4	−0.1723	−0.517
France	April '69–Sept. '69	6	−11.1094	−22.218
Germany	July '69–Nov. '69	4	+8.3953	+25.186
United Kingdom	April '69–May '69	1	−0.0276	−0.331
	Jan. '70–April '70	3	−0.0237	−0.095

SOURCE: *Federal Reserve Bulletin,* May 1970, p. A-89.

One final example of the practical meaning of small daily changes in foreign exchange values can be developed from the daily quotations from the *Wall Street Journal,* wherein an order for, say, $10,000 is quoted in terms of foreign currency on a given date and the currency received is then converted to U.S. dollars at the rate prevailing on a later date, say a month or more later. Examples are given below. Basic quotations are selling prices for bank transfers in the United States for payment abroad; the buying price of the foreign currency when it becomes due is subject to buying-selling spread as well as to differentials based on the nature and standing of the debtor.

Currencies	*April 24, 1970*	*May 25, 1970*
British pounds		
£/$US rate	$US 2.4064	$US 2.401
£ equivalent	4,155.60	
$US equivalent	10,000.00	9,977.60
Canadian dollars		
$C/$US rate	$US 0.9375	$US 0.9323
$C equivalent	10,723.90	
$US equivalent	10,000.00	9,997.89
Swiss francs		
SF/$US rate	$US 0.23265	$US 0.23185
SF equivalent	42,983	
$US equivalent	10,000.00	9,965.61

A few observations should be made before leaving these examples. First, exchange rates change daily. What may appear to be a minor change in terms of currency units can be an important percentage change. Second, foreign currency values in terms of dollars may increase and decrease within a given time period, say a year. Third, the changes indicated, other than those approved by the International Monetary Fund (IMF), are normally within the 1 percent range from established par values because of the IMF provision for government intervention to maintain rate stability. Permissible fluctuations from established parities were increased to 2.25 percent in December 1971 by agreement between the United States and other Group of Ten member countries.

What the expected range of fluctuation may be in the future was uncertain as of late 1971, but after the United States action in August terminating its sales of gold at $35 an ounce, discussions were in progress about future international monetary arrangements, including the question of the advisability of reestablishing par values.

Now, how important may all this be relative to a company's profits? We can obtain an indication by relating foreign exchange fluctuations to a few typical ratios of net profits to net sales as reported by Dun & Bradstreet. The most applicable for foreign traders appear to be those of wholesalers and manufacturing concerns, shown in Table 7. It is obvious, when considering net profits on sales, that the degree of fluctuation in foreign exchange between shipment and payment dates may offset in some cases and exceed in others the indicated net profits. This assumes, for the purpose of comparison, that if the net profit on sales overall were the same as that on sales to a given country whose foreign exchange fluctuation

Table 7. Ratio of net profits to net sales in 1969.

Number of Concerns		*Lower Quartile*	*Median*	*Upper Quartile*
	Wholesalers			
181	Automotive equipment	1.16	2.13	3.44
46	Chemicals and allied products	0.71	1.62	5.60
34	Commercial machines and equipment	0.22	1.45	2.73
148	Electrical apparatus and equipment	0.98	1.63	2.42
187	Hardware	0.72	1.48	2.53
184	Plumbing and heating equipment	0.87	1.74	3.13
	Manufacturers			
40	Agricultural chemicals	0.69	1.45	4.11
86	Construction, mining and handling machinery and equipment	2.09	3.86	6.09
59	Electric lighting and wiring equipment	1.25	2.82	4.79
71	Farm machinery and equipment	1.39	2.42	4.78
44	Household appliances	1.26	3.16	5.19
89	Special industry machinery	1.14	3.78	6.17

SOURCE: "Key Business Ratios in 125 Lines, 1969," Dun and Bradstreet, Inc., 1970.

is being observed, the two percentage ratios may be set side by side with some validity. In any case, normal foreign exchange fluctuations are not to be treated lightly and are an important factor in determining whether a price quotation is to be made in one currency or another.

The problem is that the decision as to currency to be quoted must be made on the date of offer or sale to a foreign customer. However, the choice of currency in which a transaction is to be financed is not always a free decision on the part of the exporter or importer. It may be influenced, if not dictated, by the importer's government. For example, in 1969 and 1970 Japanese importers were reported to have been pressed to finance their U.S. purchases in dollars rather than in yen because interest rates for borrowing in the United States were lower at the time than they were in Japan. To this, U.S. exporters should have no objection, but it does point up the possibility that choice of currency may come under influences other than those of the individual positions of an exporter and importer.

Trade Terms and Standardized Definitions

Over the years, international business practice and court decisions have resulted in a number of commonly used terms that contribute to a better understanding of what is meant to be included or excluded in a given price quotation. Yet these more or less standardized trade terms have not been accepted in many countries and have not entirely been incorporated into law. Furthermore, the efforts of businessmen to clarify the meaning of these terms have resulted in at least two recognized private codifications of terms. One is *International Commercial Terms (Incoterms), 1953,* developed by the International Chamber of Commerce; the other is *Revised American Foreign Trade Definitions, 1941,* adopted by a joint committee representing the Chamber of Commerce of the United States, the American Importers Association, and the National Foreign Trade Council.

The terms identified in the two codifications perform the important functions of defining the obligations of seller and buyer; specifying the exact point at which goods are to be delivered from seller to buyer; and allocating transportation, documental, and insurance costs between seller and buyer. The principal terms are listed in order of increasing responsibility of the seller as goods move along their distribution routes:

Ex (named point of origin).
f.o.b. (free on board) a named carrier, or a named point either in the country of exportation or importation, and sometimes with reference to freight as prepaid or allowed (f.o.b. to a named point in the interior of the country of destination throws more responsibility on the seller than does f.a.s. port of shipment and may throw more than would c.&f., c.i.f., or ex dock at port of importation).
f.a.s. (free along side) a vessel in a named port of shipment.
c.&f. (cost and freight) to a named point of destination.
c.i.f. (cost, insurance, and freight) to a named point of destination.
Ex dock (or ex quay) at named port of importation.

Since the privately agreed-upon meanings and definitions do not carry the force of law in themselves, it is advisable that the seller, in quoting a price, specify one of these agreements in order to clarify responsibility between himself and a prospective buyer. Acceptance of the specified definitions or trade terms as part of the contract of sale leaves no basis for misunderstanding and facilitates arbitration or legal processes.

Terms of Payment

Another important feature of a price quotation is the terms of payment. They can be referred to as credit terms because they specify particularly the time at which the buyer must pay or formally accept the obligation, to be paid later, and the type of credit instrument to be employed.

In view of the foregoing discussion of price quotations, it is evident that an international price quotation must encompass many more considerations than a domestic quotation. The elements that require specific mention, possibly because some of them are unique to international shipments, are well outlined in two articles with the same title, "How to Work Out Export Prices."[2] These specifications also provide the basis for better understanding between an exporter (or importer) and his bank, wherein instructions must be included in the application for a letter of credit and incorporated in part in the letter of credit itself (see Chapter 11).

---

[2] R. B. Spiro, in *The Techniques of Export Trade*, 1957, pp. 9–13; and J. R. Arnold, in *Foreign Trade*, May 15, 1965, pp. 5–11. Both periodicals are published by the Department of Industry, Trade, and Commerce, Ottawa, Canada.

6

Technical and Procedural Aspects: Operational

Once satisfaction has been reached on pricing, currency, and terms of payment, the procedural aspects shift from financial to operational. The principal aspects of these operational steps are covered at the beginning of the preceding chapter and in the following section, which deals with documents. The coordination of operational procedures will be discussed at the end of this chapter.

DOCUMENTS

Documents are evidence that someone has or has not done what he is supposed to do. They also give other facts, such as certification of quality, condition, or weight; compliance with government requirements; or the turning over to and receipt by a common carrier for delivery to a specified consignee. Documents come in for special attention because of the importance attached to them by banks, which accept them at face value without being obliged to verify their accuracy. On this point, Article 8 of *Uniform Customs and Practices for Documentary Credits* [1] reads in part: "In documentary credit operations, all parties concerned deal in documents and not in goods." Article 9 of the same agreement reads, in part,

> Banks assume no liability or responsibility for the form, sufficiency, accuracy, genuineness, falsification or legal effect of any documents, or for the general and/or particular conditions stipulated in the documents or superimposed thereon; nor do they assume any liability or responsibility for the description, quantity, weight, quality, condition, packing, delivery, value or existence of the goods represented thereby.

Bills of Lading

Each document itself could be the subject of detailed examination of form, content, and legal status, but in this book attention will be confined to the principal ones and then to a tabulation of their role in the international movement of merchandise. Because any one document, if missing, incorrect, or irregular, could in itself be an impediment to the smooth conduct of an international transaction, it is unwise to single out any one as *the* most important. Yet, in view of its function as a contract of affreightment and as documentary evidence of title it seems appropriate to consider the bill of lading as a most important document. To illustrate, Section 483 of the Tariff Act of 1930 reads as follows:

> For the purpose of this title
>
> (1) All merchandise imported into the United States shall be held to be the property of the person to whom the same is con-

---

[1] International Chamber of Commerce, 38 Cours Albert 1er, Paris 8, France. Adherence of United States banks to the agreement became effective in July 1963.

signed; and the holder of a bill of lading duly indorsed by the consignee therein named, or, if consigned to order, by the consignor, shall be deemed the consignee thereof. The underwriters of abandoned merchandise and the salvors of merchandise saved from a wreck at sea or on or along a coast of the United States may be regarded as the consignees.

(2) A person making entry of merchandise under the provisions of subdivision (h) or (i) of section 484 (relating to entry on carrier's certificate and on duplicate bill of lading, respectively) shall be deemed the sole consignee thereof.

A bill of lading is a contract between shipper and carrier whereby the carrier agrees to deliver the described merchandise to a named consignee, and the shipper agrees to pay for this service unless the transportation arrangement is for freight to be collected from the consignee. The conditions of liability of the carrier are specified by law or convention as well as by contract, which gives rise to the need for insurance against risks that are the responsibility of the shipper. The typical language of the bill of lading refers to packages "received in apparent good order and said to contain. . . ."

A number of types of bills of lading are in use. The major differences are between a *straight* and an *order* bill of lading, and between a *received for shipment* and *on-board* bill of lading. Straight bills of lading are simply instructions to a common carrier to deliver merchandise to a named consignee, according to the contract of affreightment, and to no one else. Such bills of lading need not be surrendered to obtain the merchandise.

Order bills, on the other hand, are negotiable and are widely used in international trade. They contain an instruction to the common carrier to deliver the merchandise to the named consignee or to his order. They may be to the order of the shipper, to the order of a bank or some other designated consignee, or simply "to order," although use of bills consigned to order of the shipper is not permitted in some countries, notably Venezuela and Bolivia. In other countries, Argentina for instance, an order bill cannot be used for shipment of arms and munitions. Because order bills are negotiable, they must be surrendered to the carrier's agent in the country of destination in order to permit him to deliver the merchandise without risk of a holder later presenting a demand for delivery.

For merchandise delivered to a dock, a receipt is issued containing information on which to base an *ocean* bill of lading. It states that the ocean carrier has received the described merchandise for shipment (perhaps by a named vessel) to a stated consignee. However, there is always a possibility that the vessel specified may not be available, so the shipment cannot be placed aboard it. This could cause delays in final shipment, and even nondelivery, so it is common practice to call for an on-board bill of lading, wherein the common carrier attests that the goods have in fact been taken aboard.

Much attention has centered on the use of a *through* bill of lading in international trade, on the theory that it would be a substantial convenience to a shipper if one bill of lading could cover all transportation from a seller's to a buyer's warehouse. Both preparation and processing of documents would appear to be simplified by the proposal but a number of practical obstacles impede its acceptance. Among these are:

1. The wording differs in bills of lading used by motor freight, rail, barge, ocean carrier, and airline companies. One reason is that liability attaching to the different common carriers is the subject of different laws, such as the Carriage of Goods by Sea Act for ocean carriers, the Interstate Commerce Act for rail and motor carriers, and such international agreements as the Warsaw Convention/Hague Protocol for air carriers.

2. Classification schedules differ among carriers. The class rate schedules designed for rail shipments are not always the same as those for ocean carriers; and there are differences for barge line shipments and air shipments. This means that items included in one class—say hand tools—of one carrier may not be included in the comparable class of another carrier. It is possible, as long as an individual item can be identified in any given class of different carriers, simply to add up the combined rates and arrive at the total cost. However, this does not permit carriers to work out joint rates on intermodal transportation, which would be expected to result in monetary saving over and above that from reduced paperwork.

Companion to this is the complication that in the filing of rates with regulatory agencies, each agency has specific legal authority to disapprove of the rates of carriers under its jurisdiction. Thus a bureaucratic spider web develops. Rails are subject to regulation by the Interstate Commerce Commission, ocean carriers by the Federal Maritime Commission, and air carriers by the Civil Aeronautics Board. Some arrangement would have to be worked out to have regulatory responsibilities coordinated on intermodal transportation.

3. The exact carrier, or even the exact shipping line, may not be known in advance of a shipment's arrival at a port, so identify-

ing the carrier may be impossible. Moreover, the consolidation of shipments at port by a foreign freight forwarder, with some resultant saving in cost to the shipper, constitutes an important link in international transportation.

4. Determination of whether the shipper or carrier is responsible or must take any specific risk is facilitated by each carrier's issuance of its own bill of lading, at which time it can be seen whether the goods were received in "apparent good order." Possibly some insurance spread could evolve to cover this situation but so far it has not.

5. Some shipments move in more than one package, and there is always the risk that one or more may be lost, damaged, or delayed. If an order were to move out in, say, three crates but somewhere along the way one became damaged or lost, any subsequent carrier would have to be able to cover his position of having received only two packages in apparent good order and one in damaged condition. There might be a question as to whether the two should go forward without waiting for the third to be repaired or replaced, and here again one sees a complication in having the shipment covered by only one bill of lading, as convenient as this might otherwise be.

6. Actual rates are often negotiated and not known in advance; they may differ according to the availability of cargo space at the time, so the setting of a through rate might be impeded, if not impossible.

Other considerations may develop but the foregoing will suffice to suggest that through bills of lading, which for best advantage to the shipper require through transportation rates, appear to be a long way off from widespread use.

The number and types of documents used vary widely, depending on the desires of sellers and buyers, on their banks, and on laws and regulations of the countries of exportation and importation. Those in most common use, apart from bills of lading, are discussed in the following pages.

Marine (Air) Insurance Policies or Certificates

These are necessary to protect a shipper against risks attaching to him in part because common carrier liability is limited by law as well as by contract.

It is not necessary for anyone studying exporting and importing, or even engaged in the operation, to know all the details about marine insurance, but as a minimum it is advisable to recognize the difference between, in insurance parlance, *general average* and *particular average*. The term *general average* is important because in international transportation by vessel, risk attaches to merchandise from causes other than loss or damage to that particular merchandise. An ocean voyage may be compared to a joint venture by all shippers and the carrier, wherein voluntary loss or damage to any one shipper's goods *for the common benefit of all* must be borne by all rather than only by the shipper whose goods were destroyed or damaged.

For example, if it became necessary to jettison cargo to lighten the ship in order to save the ship and its cargo, the shipper whose goods were thrown overboard would be reimbursed with all, including himself, contributing on a pro rata basis according to overall valuation of the cargo and ship. Or a vessel or part of the cargo may be on fire; water and steam used to extinguish the fire may damage cargo not touched by the fire. This would be a "voluntary" damage to save the entire ship and its cargo, from which the ship and the undamaged cargo benefit. Another example is the expense of floating a vessel when stranded. This joint risk is called general average, and all marine insurance policies include such coverage.

Particular average, on the other hand, pertains to loss or damage to one's specific merchandise. Under what are called "American conditions" the damage, to be covered, must be caused by the vessel's having been stranded, sunk, burned, or in collision. "European conditions" appear to be somewhat more liberal.

Commercial Invoices

In international business as well as in domestic business, an orderly monetary claim must be presented by a seller to a buyer and copies may be required by the governments of the exporting or importing company. One reason for this is exchange controls. There can be no standard form, obviously, but to accomplish its purpose a commercial invoice must spell out the price, currency, total value, discounting arrangement, and credit terms.

Consular and Special Customs Invoices

These detailed memoranda are frequently required by the governments of the importer's country. Consular invoices serve to give information from commercial invoices on a uniform basis, as far as the country of import is concerned, thus providing useful information for the assessment of import duty and at the same time yielding sworn statements of authenticity. In fact, a consular invoice may require some details that do not normally appear on a commercial invoice, and that is another reason for its use. In the United States consular invoices have been superseded by special customs invoices. The special customs invoice calls for considerably more information than one normally finds on a commercial invoice, and part of it is designed to yield information that may be used in investigations of dumping. A copy of a special customs invoice is shown in Figure 1. A set of instructions for the preparation of special customs invoices has been issued by the Bureau of Customs.

Shipper's Export Declarations

As a general rule, exporters are required to notify the Bureau of Customs when merchandise leaves the country.[2] (No duty is collectible on exports, but these reports constitute the primary data on export statistics, which serve a useful purpose in market research.) For some years, carriers were not permitted to load shipments unless the shipper's export declarations had been previously filed with a collector of customs. In order to streamline the paperwork involved in exporting, certain procedures were simplified in 1969. Under the modified arrangement, exporters can turn merchandise over to carriers prior to having the export declaration authenticated by the Bureau of Customs if the carriers agree to review the declarations for acceptability before loading and to forward them subsequently to the Bureau of Customs. In addition, high-volume exporters meeting requirements established by the Office of Export Control and the Bureau of the Census have the option of filing monthly export declarations instead of a declaration for each export shipment to Free World countries of goods whose export administration is under Department of Commerce jurisdiction. Reports can be filed in a specified written summary form or presented on computer tape or punched cards that are compatible with systems used by the Bureau of the Census.

The third step in streamlining procedures was to raise the limit below which shipper's export declarations need not be filed. Formerly it was $100 for shipments to Free World countries; now the amount is $250. It was estimated by the Department of Commerce that this change could eliminate 1½ million documents a

---

[2] See U.S. Department of Commerce, *International Commerce*, September 22, 1969, p. 6.

FIGURE 1

Special customs invoice.

TREASURY DEPARTMENT

Attach Additional Sheets Here
Read Carefully Instructions for Preparation of Invoice

Form Approved.
Budget Bureau No. 48-R342.3.

(THIS FORM DOES NOT REQUIRE CERTIFICATION BY A UNITED STATES CONSULAR OFFICER)

SPECIAL CUSTOMS INVOICE

BUREAU OF CUSTOMS

(Original only required for customs purposes)

I. THIS SECTION TO BE FILLED IN FOR EVERY SHIPMENT

1. How were goods obtained by importer? By purchase or agreement to purchase ☐ By some means other than a purchase ☐

DO NOT INCLUDE PURCHASE AND NONPURCHASE GOODS IN SAME INVOICE. USE SEPARATE INVOICE FOR EACH

2. Place (city and country) and date obtained by importer	3. Name of exporting carrier	4. Date of shipment

II. TO BE FILLED IN IF GOODS WERE PURCHASED OR AGREED TO BE PURCHASED	III. TO BE FILLED IN IF GOODS WERE *NOT* PURCHASED
1. Name and address of seller	1. Name and address of person from whom goods were obtained
2. Name and address of purchaser	2. Nam. and address of consignee
3. Date order accepted	3. Name and address of person for whose account goods are shipped

IV. THIS SECTION TO BE FILLED IN FOR EVERY SHIPMENT

(1) Marks and Numbers on Shipping Packages	(2) Manufacturer's or Seller's Numbers or Symbols	(3) Quantity and Full Description of Goods (State contents of each package and importer's numbers or symbols, if any)	(4) Invoice Unit Price or Value	(5) Invoice Totals and Show Separately Packing Costs; All Other Costs, Charges, and Expenses	(6) Current Unit Price for Home Consumption in Home Currency	(7) Current Unit Price for Export to United States

(8) Country of origin	(9) If rate of exchange is fixed or agreed, give rate	(10) If discount is freely offered, give terms, amount, and whether trade or cash

V. THIS SECTION TO BE FILLED IN FOR EVERY SHIPMENT

1. IF GOODS WERE PURCHASED, have you stated in section IV, column 4, the purchase price of each item in the currency in which the goods were bought? ☐ Yes ☐ No.
2. IF THE GOODS WERE NOT PURCHASED, have you stated in section IV, column 4, the price that you would have received or would be willing to receive now if the goods were sold in the ordinary course of trade for exportation to the United States? ☐ Yes ☐ No.
3. What currency was used in this invoice transaction? ....
4. Whether the goods were purchased or obtained by the United States importer in some other manner, have you stated in section IV, column 6:
   (A) (1) The price at which you are now selling the goods or offering them for sale for home consumption, including all applicable taxes? ☐ Yes ☐ No.
   (2) Is this price freely offered to anyone who wishes to buy the goods for home consumption? ☐ Yes ☐ No.
   (B) (1) Have you stated in section IV, column 7, the price at which you are now selling the goods or offering them for sale for export to the United States and whether this price is f.o.b., c.i.f., c.&f., or whatever the fact may be? ☐ Yes ☐ No.
   (2) Is this price freely offered to anyone who wishes to buy the goods for export to the United States? ☐ Yes ☐ No.
5. Have you listed all charges and stated whether each amount has been included in or excluded from the invoice amount? ☐ Yes ☐ No. Is the inland freight included in the invoice price or value? ☐ Yes ☐ No. Is the price or value of the goods the same at the factory as at the point of delivery? ☐ Yes ☐ No. If the answer is No, have any sales been made at an ex-factory price? ☐ Yes ☐ No.
6. Are any rebates, drawbacks, bounties, or other grants allowed upon the exportation of the goods? ☐ Yes ☐ No. If so, have all been separately itemized? ☐ Yes ☐ No.
7. If such or similar goods are being sold or offered for sale in the home market for home consumption, what taxes are applicable and are they included in the price shown in section IV, column 6?

Rate .... Kind ....

CUSTOMS FORM JUL 64 5515

SECTION V (Continued)

8. (A) Did production of goods involve costs for "assists" (i.e.—dies, molds, tooling, printing plates, patterns, drawings, blueprints, artwork, engineering work, design and development, financial assistance) ***not included*** in the invoice price?

☐ Yes ☐ No. If yes, identify nature of assist involved ...., and complete Part B.

(B) (1) Assists valued at .... were supplied by:
("Unknown," if applicable)

☐ Manufacturer ☐ Importer ☐ Other (Identify) ....

(2) Assists were: ☐ (a) Supplied without cost. ☐ (b) Supplied on rental basis.
☐ (c) Invoiced separately. If (c), attach copy of invoice.

9. If the price(s) shown in column 6 is (are) higher than those shown in column 7, there is an indication of possible sales at less than fair value within the meaning of the United States Antidumping statutes. If this differential exists, please select one of the following alternatives:

(A) ☐ To the best of my knowledge and belief the differential between the column 6 and column 7 prices is the result of conditions of sale which would not result in sales at less than fair value within the meaning of the U.S. Antidumping laws.

OR

(B) ☐ There is attached hereto an explanation of the differences between the column 6 and column 7 prices.

NOTE.—In his discretion the appraiser may nonetheless require submission of the information called for under item 9. (B).

10. PURCHASE DECLARATION	11. NONPURCHASE DECLARATION
I declare that the merchandise described in this invoice is SOLD OR AGREED TO BE SOLD; that all the information contained herein is true and correct; and that there is no other invoice(s) except	I declare that the merchandise described in this invoice is shipped OTHERWISE THAN BY PURCHASE OR AGREEMENT TO PURCHASE; that all the information contained herein is true and correct; and that there is no other invoice(s) except
Explanation of Exceptions	Explanation of Exceptions
Date / Signature of Seller, Shipper, or Agent of Either	Date / Signature of Shipper or Agent

This form of invoice required generally if rate of duty based upon or regulated by value of goods and purchase price or value of shipment exceeds $500. Otherwise, use commercial invoice.

False statements or willful omissions in any invoice or other documents executed and forwarded for United States Customs entry purposes will subject the goods to seizure and forfeiture or any person involved will be subject to a penalty equal to the value of the goods. Publicity will be given to all seizures and penalties, including the disclosure of the identity of the offenders involved (19 U.S.C. 1592).

Vague or misleading information may result in expensive trouble to importer and delays in customs clearance.

Supplies of this form may be secured from consular offices of the United States and from The Publication and Reproduction Section, 201 Varick Street, New York, N. Y. 10014. Privately printed forms must conform in all respects to the official form.

GPO 960-938

year, or almost 20 percent of the total formerly required, and that it would affect only about 1 percent of the dollar value of U.S. exports. These streamlining procedures apply only to general-license shipments moving to Free World countries (that is, those not requiring individual validated licenses). A copy of the shipper's export declaration form is shown in Figure 2.

Export Licenses

All exports from the United States are subject to control. It is United States policy to control exports to the extent necessary to protect the domestic economy from the excessive drain of scarce materials, reduce the serious inflationary impact of abnormal foreign demand, further the foreign policy of the United States, fulfill its international responsibilities, and exercise vigilance over exports from the standpoint of their significance to national security.

Depending on the products, and to some degree their intended use, jurisdiction over their exportation rests with designated government agencies. The most important agency, from the viewpoint of commercial exports, is the Department of Commerce, which exercises control over most exports from the United States. *The Quarterly Reports on Export Control,* published by the Department of Commerce, list products whose exportation is under jurisdiction of an agency other than the Department of Commerce and identify the responsible agency. Control over exports under jurisdiction of the Department of Commerce is maintained through a program that divides all country destinations (except Canada, since most exports to Canada for internal consumption require neither a validated nor a general license) into seven groups and places all commodities for which export licensing is required on a *Commodity Control List,* which identifies for each commodity the destinations for which a validated export license is needed.

For most shipments an open general license has been established, but anyone interested in exporting should appreciate the fact that exporting is legally a privilege, and not a right. However, the restrictions actually applied are undertaken to accomplish definite policy goals and in general the program operates mainly as a matter of surveillance rather than of detailed daily interference with many transactions.

Certificates of Weight or Inspection

These are primarily for the protection of the exporter or importer, who may find it advantageous to call on a third party to at-

FIGURE 2.

Shipper's export declaration form.

Form 7525-V
(Rev. July 1962)

(See Instructions on Reverse Side)

U.S. DEPARTMENT OF COMMERCE
BUREAU OF THE CENSUS—BUREAU OF INTERNATIONAL COMMERCE

SHIPPER'S EXPORT DECLARATION

OF SHIPMENTS FROM THE UNITED STATES

Export Shipments Are Subject To U.S. Customs Inspection

READ CAREFULLY THE INSTRUCTIONS ON BACK TO AVOID DELAY AT SHIPPING POINT

For shipments to foreign countries, the export declaration (*a*) must be presented to and authenticated by the Collector of Customs before the goods are placed on pier or dock or other place of loading for the purpose of exporting by water or air; (*b*) must be presented to and authenticated by the Collector prior to exportation where the goods are exported by other means.

Declarations Should Be Typewritten Or Prepared In Ink

Form approved. Budget Bureau No. 41-R397.5.

CONFIDENTIAL For use solely for official purposes authorized by the Secretary of Commerce. Use for unauthorized purposes is not permitted. (Title 15, Sec. 30.5 (b) C.F.R.; 50 U.S.C. App., 2026c.)

Customs Authentication (For Customs use only.)

Do Not Use This Area	District	Port	Country (For customs use only)

FILE NO. (For Customs use only.)

1. FROM (*U.S. Port of Export*)

2. METHOD OF TRANSPORTATION (*check one*):
☐ Vessel (incl. ferry) ☐ Air ☐ Other (*Specify*) ______

2a. EXPORTING CARRIER (*If vessel, give name of ship, flag and pier number. If air, give name of airline.*)

3. EXPORTER (*Principal or seller—licensee*) ADDRESS (*Number, street, place, state*)

4. AGENT OF EXPORTER (*Forwarding agent*) ADDRESS (*Number, street, place, state*)

5. ULTIMATE CONSIGNEE ADDRESS (*Place, country*)

6. INTERMEDIATE CONSIGNEE ADDRESS (*Place, country*)

7. FOREIGN PORT OF UNLOADING (*For vessel and air shipments only*)

8. PLACE AND COUNTRY OF ULTIMATE DESTINATION (*Not place of transshipment*)

(9) MARKS AND NOS.	(10) NUMBER AND KIND OF PACKAGES, DESCRIPTION OF COMMODITIES, EXPORT LICENSE NUMBER, EXPIRATION DATE (OR GENERAL LICENSE SYMBOL) (Describe commodities in sufficient detail to permit verification of the Schedule B commodity numbers assigned. Do not use general terms. Insert required license information on line below description of each item)	(11) SHIPPING (*Gross*) WEIGHT IN POUNDS [a] (required for vessel and air shipments only)	(12) SPECIFY "D" OR "F" [b]	(13) SCHEDULE B COMMODITY NO.	(14) NET QUANTITY IN SCHEDULE B UNITS (*State unit*)	(15) VALUE AT U. S. PORT OF EXPORT (Selling price or cost if not sold, including inland freight, insurance and other charges to U. S. port of export) (*Nearest whole dollar; omit cents figures*)

16. WAYBILL OR MANIFEST NO. (*of Exporting Carrier*)

17. DATE OF EXPORTATION (*Not required for shipments by vessel*)

18. THE UNDERSIGNED HEREBY AUTHORIZES ______ (Name and address—Number, street, place, State) TO ACT AS FORWARDING AGENT FOR EXPORT CONTROL AND CUSTOMS PURPOSES.

EXPORTER ______ BY (DULY AUTHORIZED OFFICER OR EMPLOYEE) ______

▶ 19. I CERTIFY THAT ALL STATEMENTS MADE AND ALL INFORMATION CONTAINED IN THIS EXPORT DECLARATION ARE TRUE AND CORRECT. I AM AWARE OF THE PENALTIES PROVIDED FOR FALSE REPRESENTATION. (*See Paragraphs I (c), (e), on reverse side.*)

Signature ______ (Duly authorized officer or employee of exporter or named forwarding agent) For ______ (Name of corporation or firm, and capacity of signer; e.g., secretary, export manager, etc.)

Address ______

▶ Declaration should be made by duly authorized officer or employee of exporter or of forwarding agent named by exporter.

[a] If shipping weight is not available for each Schedule B item listed in column (13) included in one or more packages, insert the approximate gross weight for each Schedule B item. The total of these estimated weights should equal the actual weight of the entire package or packages.

[b] Designate foreign merchandise (reexports) with an "F" and exports of domestic merchandise produced in the United States or changed in condition in the United States with a "D." (*See instructions on reverse side.*)

CARRIERS, FORWARDERS AND EXPORTERS ARE REMINDED THAT IF A DESTINATION CONTROL STATEMENT IS REQUIRED ON A SHIPPER'S EXPORT DECLARATION COVERING A GIVEN SHIPMENT, SUCH STATEMENT MUST ALSO APPEAR ON ALL COPIES OF THE BILL OF LADING AND COMMERCIAL INVOICE. (*See Comprehensive Export Schedule.*)

Do Not Use This Area

test to a shipment's possessing certain characteristics such as quality or condition. This may be necessary in buying from samples, by classification, or from someone not well known to the buyer. Such a procedure is usually at the behest of the buyer or potential importer, so the expense is usually borne by him.[3]

Certificates of Origin

Certificates of origin are usually required by governments for determining whether merchandise presented for importation is subject to regulation or debarring for some reason or other. This could be the case if the merchandise were subject to quantitative limitations, if it were the product of an enemy country, or if it came from a region or country where there were some disease that might be transmitted by products originating there. Probably the greatest current interest in certificates of origin, however, is related to rates of duty. The world is now something of a honeycomb of special and preferential duty arrangements. Merchandise originating in one place may be subject to no duty at all (as in the case of intratrade of free trade associations), while the same merchandise would be subject to duty if it originated outside the preferred countries.

Similarly, merchandise whose import is subject to quantitative limitations would be a prime candidate for the use of a certificate of origin as proof of its eligibility for import. There are other situations suggesting use of certificates of origin but the few mentioned here should suffice to indicate their growing importance, both to exporters and to importers, and to the importer's government.

Import Entry

The form of this document varies, depending on the type of entry made, but one form must be filed with the Bureau of Customs when merchandise is brought into U.S. customs territory. Regulations as to the several types of entry permitted are provided in *Customs Regulations of the United States,* issued by the Treasury Department.

Many documents other than those mentioned are used in international trade, and it would be practically impossible to catalog

[3] See *Revised American Foreign Trade Definitions, 1941* (available from the National Foreign Trade Council, the Chamber of Commerce of the United States, the American Importers Association, and most major banks engaged in financing foreign trade).

them all. For practical and general applicability, however, the foregoing will suffice. To summarize, these documents and their common applicability are shown in Table 8.

COORDINATING MOVEMENT OF GOODS

The principal steps that are involved in an international shipment by ocean carrier have been identified. They cannot all be done at once because some are sequential to others. Yet they must all be done in time to permit shipment (sometimes turning over to the ocean vessel) by an expected or explicitly stated date, with the interest of seller and buyer protected every step of the way in which they bear risk. Eventually, also, a bank's interest may enter into consideration, as will that of certain governmental regulatory agencies.

It is costly and inefficient to have merchandise jam up transportation facilities at port by arriving before complete, integrated handling arrangements have been made. And it is even worse to have merchandise arrive too late or to have it held up and unable to move on because of documentary shortcomings. This could cause it to miss a sailing. At the very least it presents a problem to the steamship operator, who prefers to load his cargo according to destination—first on, last off.

For this reason, delivery permits from the steamship line are required before the goods will be accepted by the carrier's agent at the pier. If the merchandise arrives far enough in advance and is not unloaded from, say, a railroad car within the time specified, a shipper becomes subject to a demurrage charge. If it is unloaded and the ocean carrier is not ready for it or is unable to accept it because of documentary deficiencies or because its vessel is not yet in port, the shipment may become subject to storage charges. So, figuratively, as in making a cake, the ingredients must be put together at the right time and in the right place, just before placing the cake in the preheated oven. Thus it is obvious that international shipments require extensive planning and coordination.

Another imperative to good coordination and planning of international shipments is that in certain countries one may be fined if merchandise arrives before the documents do. Moreover, documents, some of which may only be available after a prior procedural step, must be collected and sent together to be made available to the importer or his bank or representative upon their performance of specified and prearranged action, such as paying or

Table 8. Principal documents and their functions in international trade (product identification on each).

	Bill of Lading	*Insurance Policy of Certificate*	*Commercial Invoice*	*Consular or Special Customs Invoice*	*Shipper's Export Declaration*	*Export License*	*Certificate of Weight, Condition, Inspection, etc.*	*Certificate of Origin*	*Import Entry*
Evidencing:	Receipt for shipment, or shipment by: Certain date; Certain line; Certain vessel	Cover against risks: General; Particular	Quantity; Price or value; Currency in which payable; Credit terms	Quantity; Price or value (useful in determining applicable import duty)	Quantity; Value; Identity of exporter and consignee; Foreign port of unloading; Ultimate destination; Manner of transport; Weight; Statistical classification (serves as primary source of export statistics)	Right to export	Product characteristics as specified	Country of origin (useful in determining applicable duty rate, and in import control programs)	Quantity; Value; Identity of exporter and importer; Foreign port of loading; Country of origin; Statistical classification; Weight; Estimated duty (serves as basis of duty; also as primary source of import statistics)
Useful to or required by:									
Exporter's government			(1)		√	√	(2)		
Exporter	√	√	√	(3)	√	√	(3)	√	
Importer	√	√	√	√		√	√	√	√
Importer's government	√		√	√			(4)	√	√
Common carrier	√	√			√	√			

(1) May be for exchange control purposes. (2) In few specific cases. (3) Required of rather than by. (4) As affects health and sanitary regulations.

accepting a draft. Presenting documents for certification may be possible only during a few hours a day, and they may be processed and returned only after another couple of days' delay, so all these bottlenecks must be known, anticipated, and scheduled for accommodation in ample time to have merchandise and documents move forward in synchronized, desired time, a process dictated largely by the procedural steps through which each must go.

7

Identifying Foreign Market Opportunities

After a general orientation to distribution channels, organization for exporting, and some of the technical and procedural aspects involved in carrying out international trade transactions, the next step is practical application. Assuming that a company has become attracted to venturing into foreign markets, the principal question is where? Therefore, the next focus is inquiry into methods of narrowing the world down to specific foreign markets and identifying where foreign market opportunities appear to be.

Nature of the Product

Starting with one's product, knowledge of its uses and users, and a general knowledge of the world, one is fairly able to know whether a particular country or geographic area is a possibility, whether a limited group of isolated customers in different parts of the world should be approached individually, or whether customers are numerous and are not to be approached individually by the exporter. As indications of how the nature of the product will delineate geography for this purpose, consider that wearing apparel, desired for style or function, must relate to climate and standard of living in the foreign market. Special-purpose machinery, such as for coal mining, is useful only where coal mines are located. And a few governments or large contractors will be the only export targets for certain unique items, such as the aerospace programs.

Avenues of Approach

Many service organizations may contribute to the initial selection of a foreign market for investigation. Among these are transportation companies, ports, trade associations, and chambers of commerce and similar promotional undertakings. Firms in the same line of business or firms selling to the same type of customer as those to which a potential exporter would sell are also a key to opening doors to export markets.

Still another avenue is published trade opportunities, such as those appearing in *Commerce Today*, a weekly published by the U.S. Department of Commerce, or in the private publications of ports, international airlines, various steamship companies, or chambers of commerce in American cities. These opportunities have the advantage of identifying not only a country but individuals or firms within that country who are seeking American connections. Other approaches can be tried, such as professional service facilities, including combination export managers, advertising firms, consulting firms, and market research firms.

INTERNATIONAL TRADE STATISTICS

One of the most important ways of identifying foreign markets is to use international trade statistics. Here is the official story of transactions in merchandise between importing countries and exporting countries of any statistically identifiable product in international trade. However, one must be able to relate his product as closely as possible to the statistical classification available, and this involves some knowledge of statistical systems and of the availability of current data.

In the abstract, if international trade statistics show significant imports of a given product (or product type) into any country, it can be taken as reliable evidence that local production is inadequate to meet demand, and that trade restrictions can be overcome by *some* exporters, who may or may not be in a preferred position. Moreover, if United States trade statistics show that the product in which we are interested is exported from the United States, foreign markets for U.S. production exist, and some United States producers and exporters are competitive in at least some world markets.

U.S. Export Statistics

The primary reference for statistics on U.S. exports is Report FT410 (*U.S. Exports, Schedule B, Commodity by Country of Destination*). This is a monthly publication of the Bureau of the Census, covering U.S. exports of some 3,600 products in commodity detail as fine as seven-digit codes, in terms of Schedule B (Revised, 1965). The publications are issued approximately 9 to 12 weeks after the close of the month, and include data for that month and cumulative statistics for the year to date. The December issue, whose cumulative column constitutes the annual total, becomes available some time in March of the following year. It is therefore the record for a very recent period.

If we select a product at random, say outboard motors, (#7115030), we see that in 1969, U.S. exports went to the foreign markets indicated in Table 9. As a basis for the most reliable analysis and conclusions, comparable data for the last two or three years should be examined in case of inconsistency in volumes in any one year.

Some of the exports to certain destinations appearing in the table are substantial in amount: eight are over $1 million and nine more are between $500,000 and $999,000. But the data shown represent only exports from the United States (in each case, at least three exporters are covered; statistics are not released if their confidentiality may be violated by identifying or permitting someone to identify their supplier), and one must be interested in his competition from all areas. So the question is where competition lies insofar as exports from other countries are concerned.

Table 9. Exports of outboard motors from the United States, 1969 (Schedule B # 7115030).

Country	*Value ($000)*	*Country*	*Value ($000)*
Canada	147	Spain	232
Mexico	1,021	Portugal	261
Guatemala	91	Malta	15
British Honduras	34	Italy	1,263
El Salvador	52	Yugoslavia	16
Honduras	41	Greece	87
Nicaragua	48	Turkey	55
Costa Rica	80	Cyprus	17
Panama	269	Iraq	19
Bermuda	29	Iran	26
Bahamas	405	Israel	19
Jamaica	184	Kuwait	33
Dominican Republic	44	Arabia	59
Leeward & Windward Is.	47	India	18
N. Antilles	118	Pakistan	75
French West Indies	172	Ceylon	109
Colombia	514	Thailand	50
Venezuela	1,364	Singapore	114
Guyana	52	Indonesia	224
Surinam	12	Philippines	158
French Guiana	66	Korea	40
Ecuador	90	Hong Kong	50
Peru	87	Japan	1,112
Bolivia	27	Australia	1,026
Chile	53	New Zealand	273
Brazil	991	Br. W. Pacific Is.	15
Paraguay	43	Fr. Pacific Is.	175
Uruguay	64	Tr. Terr. Pacific Is.	214
Argentina	799	Morocco	87
Sweden	2,259	Algeria	22
Norway	1,035	Ivory Coast	23
Finland	614	Ghana	100
Denmark	606	Nigeria	103
United Kingdom	866	Angola	59
Netherlands	479	Congo	86
Belgium	275	Ethiopia	22
France	1,209	Kenya	81
West Germany	999	Mozambique	92
Austria	129	Republic of South Africa	594
Switzerland	266	Zambia	41
		Other countries	174
		Total	23,129

SOURCE: U.S. Department of Commerce, *Foreign Trade,* FT410. December 1969.

Statistics of Other Countries

There are at least three sources to which one may turn for such intelligence. First is the *import* statistics of countries to which someone from the U.S. is already an exporter. A real problem, here, however, is the accessibility, comparability, timeliness, detail, and possibly translation of their statistics. A second source of such intelligence is United States *import* statistics to the extent the product is imported into the United States and is identifiable in *Tariff Schedules of the United States, Annotated* (TSUSA), the import classification system. This system contains approximately 10,000 product identifications. Detailed data so collected are available for reference in unpublished monthly aggregations as well as in certain published reports.

The published report from which the information is available is FT135 (*U.S. Imports, Schedule A, Commodity Classification by Country of Origin*). Like its counterpart on exports (FT410), this is also a monthly publication, with the annual totals in the December report, which is cumulative from January. By reference to the *export* statistics of the countries that are our principal suppliers, again subject to the ability to identify the product in their statistics, it is possible to identify the countries other than the United States to which they export.

Statistical Publications of International Organizations

The third source of trade statistics of other countries is statistical publications of international organizations. These publications use standard nomenclature but their reports are not as detailed as some of the national statistical systems. The Standard International Trade Classification (SITC) is the language employed by some 70 countries for reporting their foreign trade statistics. These data are the best available, internationally, but a constant and practical question is whether SITC is sufficiently precise to cover one's product. It contains only 1,312 statistical codes as against some 3,600 for the U.S. Schedule B Export Classification, and some complaints are heard that even Schedule B does not give enough detail. The difficulty lies in being able to relate the foreign trade of one's own specific product(s) with that of a basket category; for example, SITC item 861.9(3) covers "drawing, measuring, calculating instruments, etc."; and item 695.2(2) includes "pliers, pincers, spanners, wrenches, metal cutting shears, files, rasps, etc." From this type of grouping, one could not determine data for more specific product reference.

Now, it is fine to know the structure of statistics, or the system. But that is something like knowing only the rules of the game. The system itself is not the desired collection and reporting of numerical data, which are processed and released periodically per schedule. For this we must turn to publications or other releases of collected data according to the understood system. Commodity trade data are published in SITC terms by several international organizations, among them the United Nations, the Organization for Economic Cooperation and Development (OECD), and the European Economic Community (EEC). The publication of the OECD[1] is the most useful for preliminary identification of possible export opportunities.

This publication comes out semiannually, but for many purposes, at least initially, the annual figures are all that are needed. In other words, in attempting to identify foreign market opportunities, one should spend no time on the semiannual data unless it is to see whether there is an apparent seasonal characteristic of the reported trade. The statistics reported are at 3-, 4-, and 5-digit levels and cover a little over 700 products or product groupings. These reports become available some nine to ten months after the fact, that is, data for 1969 became available in September 1970. As indicated in Figure 3, the export tabulation shows the reporting exporting countries across the top of the page, while countries of destination are listed in the left column. Transactions are reported country by country, in thousands of U.S. dollars; however, where, for a given commodity, no reporting country shows a value of trade with a particular destination exceeding either $U.S. 100,000 or 10 percent of that country's total trade in the commodity, trade with the destination is not printed.

A limitation to this publication's usefulness is that individual countries of destination are not shown for about 400 SITC 4-digit subgroups covered in the report, which gives destination data for only about 230 4-digit subgroups plus a selection of over 90 5-digit items. The same kind of data are available on imports into the same reporting countries, with some minor differences in product coverage. Figure 4 shows the layout for reporting import statistics on the same product (electromechanical hand tools with self-con-

---

[1] Organization for Economic Cooperation and Development (2 rue André-Pascal, Paris 16), *OECD Commodity Trade: Exports* and *OECD Commodity Trade: Imports, Series C.*

FIGURE 3.

Commodity trade data (exports of reporting countries).

EXPORTS (f.o.b.)

VALUES
(1000 U.S. dollars)

January-December 1969

729.6 ELECTRO-MECHANICAL HAND TOOLS — OUTILS ET MACHINES-OUTILS ELECTROMECAN. A MAIN 729.6

TRADE WITH ↓ / REPORTING COUNTRIES ⇨	O.E.C.D. TOTAL	Canada	United States	Japan	O.E.C.D. EUROPE	E.E.C.	Belgium-Luxembourg	Netherlands	Germany	France	Italy	E.F.T.A.	United Kingdom
WORLD	158137	3441	23549	9163	121984	74807	569	6482	58115	2680	6961	46946	21629
OECD TOTAL	125835	3273	15838	4784	101940	63170	546	6028	49738	1515	5343	38623	16226
CANADA	12757	.	10790	46	1921	787	.	.	778	3	6	1134	892
UNITED STATES	11383	3191	.	3603	4589	2150	8	19	2095	7	21	2418	390
JAPAN	2163	43	1080	.	1040	733	.	.	663	.	70	307	273
OECD EUROPE	99532	39	3968	1135	94390	59500	538	6009	46202	1505	5246	34764	14671
EEC	60016	6	2518	733	56759	33577	478	3885	25317	1008	2889	23120	9045
EFTA	33519	33	1237	260	31989	22205	49	2006	18151	180	1819	9720	4605
AUSTRIA	6014	.	52	10	5952	4479	3	420	3558	13	485	1473	719
BELGIUM/LUXEMB.	7966	1	294	28	7643	5894	.	547	4584	502	261	1749	1243
DENMARK	5081	.	66	10	5005	3039	4	301	2541	1	192	1966	861
FINLAND	1679	.	13	19	1647	925	.	215	630	6	74	722	336
FRANCE	20605	1	429	262	19913	15355	156	2660	11430	.	1109	4510	1652
GERMANY	15890	1	528	207	15154	2145	102	574	.	343	1126	12997	3908
GREECE	1302	.	30	59	1213	930	.	48	563	72	247	283	189
IRELAND	689	.	1	.	688	189	2	18	167	2	.	499	445
ITALY	6024	1	50	213	5760	4756	3	104	4588	61	.	1002	128
NETHERLANDS	9531	2	1217	23	8289	5427	217	.	4715	102	393	2862	2114
NORWAY	2538	.	16	.	2522	1601	.	138	1420	1	42	921	444
PORTUGAL	1371	.	11	1	1359	937	1	13	654	63	206	390	274
SPAIN	3617	.	134	78	3405	2389	1	50	1855	229	254	1016	312
SWEDEN	6316	1	115	27	6173	3593	.	314	2988	11	280	2580	1444
SWITZERLAND	6215	1	202	32	5980	5350	37	376	4614	49	274	629	527
TURKEY	318	.	47	5	266	204	8	1	145	14	36	62	18
UNITED KINGDOM	4305	31	762	161	3351	2281	4	229	1746	36	266	1039	.
OTHER COUNTRIES	71	.	1	.	70	6	.	1	4	.	1	64	57
NON-OECD,TOTAL	32232	165	7713	4378	19976	11577	23	453	8377	1165	1559	8316	5400
SINO-SOVIET	1348	.	.	12	1336	1074	1	24	763	8	278	262	67
POLAND	211	.	.	.	211	157	.	1	46	1	109	54	36
CZECHOSLOVAKIA	647	.	.	.	647	530	.	1	507	1	21	117	28
OTHER COUNTRIES	490	.	.	12	478	387	1	22	210	6	148	91	3
AUST/N.ZEAL/S.AFR	9438	85	1576	1058	6719	2820	1	203	2203	28	385	3880	2842
AUSTRALIA	3790	54	550	604	2582	1134	.	126	815	.	193	1433	1027
NEW ZEALAND	975	17	122	165	671	160	.	14	146	.	.	511	477
SOUTH AFRICA	4673	14	904	289	3466	1526	1	63	1242	28	192	1936	1338
LESS DEV.NON-OECD	21446	80	6137	3308	11921	7683	21	226	5411	1129	896	4174	2491
YUGOSLAVIA	1947	.	8	1	1938	1364	.	45	1240	2	77	574	13
ALGERIA	391	.	.	.	391	316	.	2	55	246	13	75	6
ANGOLA	216	.	15	2	199	98	.	2	53	19	24	101	67
KENYA	232	.	19	1	212	32	.	4	23	.	5	180	177
MEXICO	1808	3	1319	15	471	318	.	.	311	.	7	153	31
JAMAICA	225	28	126	.	71	.	.	.	.	.	.	71	71
BR.TERR AM.NES	247	6	175	.	66	14	.	.	.	.	14	52	52
COLOMBIA	521	.	441	.	80	31	.	.	31	.	.	43	3
VENEZUELA	1300	5	1006	10	279	224	.	4	171	1	48	49	10
PERU	198	.	108	13	77	47	.	1	31	10	5	30	20
BRAZIL	1781	.	652	48	1081	858	.	2	785	.	71	223	98
CHILE	437	.	151	18	268	168	.	.	138	21	9	96	79
ARGENTINA	908	.	336	18	554	330	.	6	215	23	86	223	183
THAILAND	1155	.	63	895	197	116	.	.	109	1	6	81	50
MALAYSIA	228	.	12	126	90	39	.	2	27	5	5	51	19
SINGAPORE	315	.	13	111	191	84	.	1	69	1	13	107	94
SOUTH KOREA	509	.	77	409	23	19	.	.	16	3	.	4	.
CHINA TAIWAN	1005	.	27	958	20	19	.	.	19	.	.	1	1
HONG KONG	498	.	79	131	288	143	.	12	110	7	14	145	90
PHILIPPINES	309	.	116	78	115	55	.	.	55	.	.	60	54
ISRAEL	902	4	116	48	734	397	2	53	265	17	60	337	229
IRAN	822	.	31	20	771	660	1	1	569	3	86	111	49
U.S. DEP.-OCEANIA	160	.	16	144	.	.	.	.	.	.	.	.	.
OTHER COUNTRIES	5332	34	1231	262	3805	2351	18	91	1119	770	353	1407	1095

TRADE WITH ↓ / REPORTING COUNTRIES ⇨	Norway	Sweden	Denmark	Finland	Austria	Switzerland	Portugal	Iceland	Ireland	Spain	Greece	Turkey	Yugoslavia
WORLD	36	1682	292	16	324	22918	49	.	NA	231	.	.	112
OECD TOTAL	33	1329	281	16	249	20456	33	.	.	147	.	.	86
CANADA	.	9	.	.	.	233	.	.	.	.	.	.	.
UNITED STATES	.	26	1	.	2	1999	.	.	.	21	.	.	.
JAPAN	2	22	.	.	.	10	.	.	.	.	.	.	.
OECD EUROPE	31	1272	280	16	247	18214	33	.	.	126	.	.	86
EEC	3	553	60	8	192	13226	33	.	.	62	.	.	.
EFTA	28	626	217	8	52	4184	.	.	.	64	.	.	84
AUSTRIA	1	44	3	1	.	705	.	.	.	.	.	.	2
BELGIUM/LUXEMB.	.	29	5	.	.	472	.	.	.	.	.	.	.
DENMARK	4	208	.	1	1	891	.	.	.	.	.	.	.
FINLAND	1	156	35	.	.	194	.	.	.	.	.	.	.
FRANCE	.	57	3	.	15	2783	.	.	.	48	.	.	.
GERMANY	2	316	41	5	162	8533	30	.	.	12	.	.	.
GREECE	.	14	2	.	1	77	.	.	.	.	.	.	.
IRELAND	.	.	.	.	.	54	.	.	.	.	.	.	.
ITALY	.	29	6	1	1	837	.	.	.	2	.	.	.
NETHERLANDS	1	122	5	2	14	601	3	.	.	.	.	.	.
NORWAY	.	125	66	1	1	284	.	.	.	.	.	.	.
PORTUGAL	.	4	1	.	1	110	.	.	.	32	.	.	.
SPAIN	.	46	.	.	2	656	.	.	.	.	.	.	.
SWEDEN	19	.	106	4	3	1004	.	.	.	.	.	.	.
SWITZERLAND	1	57	3	1	40	.	.	.	.	1	.	.	82
TURKEY	.	28	.	.	.	16	.	.	.	.	.	.	2
UNITED KINGDOM	2	32	3	.	6	996	.	.	.	31	.	.	.
OTHER COUNTRIES	.	5	1	.	.	1	.	.	.	.	.	.	.
NON-OECD,TOTAL	4	351	10	.	71	2465	15	.	.	83	.	.	26
SINO-SOVIET	.	24	.	.	58	113	.	.	.	.	.	.	.
POLAND	.	10	.	.	4	4	.	.	.	.	.	.	.
CZECHOSLOVAKIA	.	8	.	.	35	46	.	.	.	.	.	.	.
OTHER COUNTRIES	.	6	.	.	19	63	.	.	.	.	.	.	.
AUST/N.ZEAL/S.AFR	.	43	.	.	.	995	.	.	.	19	.	.	.
AUSTRALIA	.	39	.	.	.	367	.	.	.	15	.	.	.
NEW ZEALAND	.	.	.	.	.	34	.	.	.	.	.	.	.
SOUTH AFRICA	.	4	.	.	.	594	.	.	.	4	.	.	.
LESS DEV.NON-OECD	4	284	10	.	13	1357	15	.	.	64	.	.	26
YUGOSLAVIA	.	117	.	.	5	439	.	.	.	.	.	.	.
ALGERIA	.	11	.	.	.	58	.	.	.	.	.	.	.
ANGOLA	.	1	.	.	.	21	12	.	.	.	.	.	.
KENYA	.	.	.	.	.	3	.	.	.	.	.	.	.
MEXICO	.	14	.	.	.	108	.	.	.	.	.	.	.
JAMAICA	.	.	.	.	.	.	.	.	.	.	.	.	.
BR.TERR AM.NES	.	.	.	.	.	.	.	.	.	.	.	.	.
COLOMBIA	.	1	.	.	.	39	.	.	.	6	.	.	5
VENEZUELA	.	.	2	.	.	37	.	.	.	6	.	.	.
PERU	.	.	.	.	.	10	.	.	.	.	.	.	.
BRAZIL	.	8	.	.	.	117	.	.	.	.	.	.	.
CHILE	.	1	.	.	.	16	.	.	.	4	.	.	.
ARGENTINA	.	3	.	.	.	37	.	.	.	1	.	.	.
THAILAND	.	13	.	.	3	15	.	.	.	.	.	.	.
MALAYSIA	.	7	.	.	.	25	.	.	.	.	.	.	.
SINGAPORE	.	2	.	.	.	11	.	.	.	.	.	.	.
SOUTH KOREA	.	3	1	.	.	.	.	.	.	.	.	.	.
CHINA TAIWAN	.	.	.	.	.	.	.	.	.	.	.	.	.
HONG KONG	.	10	3	.	.	42	.	.	.	.	.	.	.
PHILIPPINES	.	2	.	.	.	4	.	.	.	.	.	.	.
ISRAEL	.	4	1	.	.	103	.	.	.	.	.	.	.
IRAN	.	15	1	.	.	46	.	.	.	.	.	.	3
U.S. DEP.-OCEANIA	.	.	.	.	.	.	.	.	.	.	.	.	.
OTHER COUNTRIES	4	72	2	.	5	226	3	.	.	47	.	.	18

FIGURE 4.

Commodity trade data (imports of reporting countries).

IMPORTS (c.i.f.)

VALUES
(1000 U.S. dollars)

January-December 1969

729.6 ELECTRO-MECHANICAL HAND TOOLS — OUTILS ET MACHINES-OUTILS ELECTROMECAN. A MAIN 729.6

REPORTING COUNTRIES ⇨ / TRADE WITH ⬇	O.E.C.D. TOTAL c.i.f./f.o.b.	Canada f.o.b.	United States f.o.b.	Japan	O.E.C.D. EUROPE	E.E.C.	Belgium-Luxembourg	Netherlands	Germany	France	Italy	E.F.T.A.	United Kingdom	Norway	Sweden	Denmark	Finland	Austria	Switzerland	Portugal	Iceland	Ireland	Spain	Greece	Turkey	Yugoslavia
WORLD	137029	26774	8547	2268	99440	58342	8014	8346	15935	20036	6011	34512	5047	2273	7163	5775	1526	5106	6095	1527	77	816	3609	1547	537	1626
OECD TOTAL	135337	26740	8466	2259	97872	58017	7915	8286	15881	19939	5996	33567	4225	2273	7147	5772	1525	5080	6021	1524	77	815	3607	1521	268	1535
CANADA	3215	.	3100	60	55	17	.	5	10	2	.	38	6	.	3	19	10	.	.	.	.	.	.	.	.	.
UNITED STATES	30754	23272	.	1352	6130	4061	493	716	1032	1413	407	1598	689	43	145	94	49	88	447	43	9	10	315	86	51	6
JAPAN	5362	464	2817	.	2081	1327	37	306	398	370	216	594	353	7	68	50	23	17	70	6	.	4	76	70	10	4
OECD EUROPE	96006	3004	2549	847	89606	52612	7385	7259	14441	18154	5373	31337	3177	2223	6931	5609	1443	4975	5504	1475	68	801	3216	1365	207	1525
EEC	57559	653	1680	504	54722	30901	5792	4917	2115	13759	4318	20214	2126	1406	3435	2898	861	3734	4696	1058	11	167	2203	1062	164	1189
EFTA	38294	2351	863	343	34737	21651	1592	2340	12318	4346	1055	11039	1003	817	3496	2711	582	1241	808	381	57	634	1010	303	43	336
AUSTRIA	363	10	.	2	351	212	5	41	159	5	2	136	3	1	.	1	.	.	130	1	.	1	1	1	.	23
BELGIUM/LUXEMB.	622	.	.	1	621	537	.	308	98	109	22	64	6	.	1	3	7	14	31	2	.	6	2	.	12	23
DENMARK	187	.	1	.	186	33	11	7	13	2	.	148	5	63	41	.	8	5	6	20	1	.	1	3	.	.
FRANCE	1604	8	2	1	1593	1048	558	107	295	.	88	205	68	4	2	3	15	8	37	68	.	.	254	76	10	1
GERMANY	43301	632	1671	398	40600	22613	4414	4019	.	10082	4098	15562	1523	1177	2751	2093	520	2838	4075	585	9	146	1555	616	99	1064
IRELAND	39	.	5	.	34	2	1	1	.	.	.	29	29	.	.	.	.	.	.	.	.	.	3	.	.	.
ITALY	6368	3	4	104	6257	3115	258	483	1158	1216	.	2453	234	63	400	468	110	519	270	389	.	3	339	316	31	77
NETHERLANDS	5664	10	3	.	5651	3588	562	.	564	2352	110	1930	295	162	281	331	209	355	283	14	2	12	53	54	12	24
SPAIN	113	.	1	.	112	58	.	1	8	49	.	54	18	.	.	.	.	.	.	36	.	.	.	.	.	.
SWEDEN	1103	130	104	2	867	440	30	63	192	71	84	374	41	26	.	157	63	29	53	5	1	5	25	3	19	18
SWITZERLAND	17867	241	473	44	17109	12593	477	587	7871	2838	820	3846	951	253	935	814	190	626	.	77	2	31	554	75	8	270
UNITED KINGDOM	18713	1958	284	294	16177	8363	1067	1637	4082	1430	147	6498	.	473	2493	1735	321	580	618	278	53	597	429	221	16	25
OTHER COUNTRIES	62	12	1	1	48	10	2	5	1	.	2	38	4	1	27	4	.	1	1	.	.	.	.	.	.	.
NON-OECD, TOTAL	1692	34	83	11	1564	323	98	59	54	98	14	941	818	.	16	2	1	27	74	3	.	3	4	25	268	89
SINO-SOVIET	648	.	.	.	648	301	98	59	45	93	6	50	4	.	15	2	.	27	2	.	.	.	4	25	268	89
USSR	52	.	.	.	52	16	7	.	.	4	5	.	.	.	.	.	.	.	.	.	.	.	.	1	35	13
GERMANY SOV. ZONE	288	.	.	.	288	152	45	57	.	50	.	16	.	.	3	1	.	11	1	.	.	.	.	13	107	70
POLAND	47	.	.	.	47	3	.	.	3	.	.	.	.	.	.	.	.	.	.	.	.	.	.	8	36	1
CZECHOSLOVAKIA	244	.	.	.	244	129	46	2	41	39	1	31	1	.	12	1	.	16	1	.	.	.	4	3	77	5
OTHER COUNTRIES	17	.	.	.	17	1	.	.	1	.	.	3	3	.	.	.	.	.	.	.	.	.	.	.	13	.
AUST/N.ZEAL/S.AFR	45	.	.	11	34	4	.	.	1	.	3	30	30	.	.	.	.	.	.	.	.	.	.	.	.	.
OTHER COUNTRIES	45	.	.	11	34	4	.	.	1	.	3	30	30	.	.	.	.	.	.	.	.	.	.	.	.	.
LESS DEV.NON-OECD	999	34	83	.	882	18	.	.	8	5	5	861	784	.	1	.	1	.	72	3	.	3	.	.	.	.
YUGOSLAVIA	87	.	.	.	87	3	.	.	.	.	3	84	12	.	.	.	.	.	72	.	.	.	.	.	.	.
INDIA	431	34	1	.	396	.	.	.	.	.	.	396	396	.	.	.	.	.	.	.	.	.	.	.	.	.
CHINA TAIWAN	27	.	27	.	.	.	.	.	.	.	.	.	.	.	.	.	.	.	.	.	.	.	.	.	.	.
HONG KONG	430	.	55	.	375	.	.	.	.	.	.	372	367	.	1	.	1	.	.	3	.	3	.	.	.	.
OTHER COUNTRIES	24	.	.	.	24	15	.	.	8	5	2	9	9	.	.	.	.	.	.	.	.	.	.	.	.	.

tained electric motors (SITC 729.6), otherwise described as hand tools, with self-contained electric motor) as that on which exports were reported in Figure 4.

The United Nations Statistical Office collects data from as many countries as are in a position to and willing to report. Special runs or tabulations designed to specification of the purchaser are available.

Market Share Reports

Probably the most significant step in providing statistical data for identifying export opportunities was undertaken by the Department of Commerce in 1963 in the conception and development of its *Market Share Reports*. This could not have been done until there was widespread reporting of foreign trade statistics on a uniform basis, that is, until the SITC came into existence and wide use. A number of countries had begun to report on this basis a year or so earlier. At present, processing of the data for the Department of Commerce is by contract with the Statistical Office of the United Nations.

The basic concept of the *Market Share Reports* concerns a given country's share of another country's import market in any given product, assuming it to be identifiable in international trade statistics. The original intent was to develop a dependable and continuing flow of intelligence on the comparative performance of American exporters in world markets and to use this intelligence as a guide for directing and expanding trade promotion efforts and as a practical aid for stimulating private interest in the opportunities disclosed through appropriate analysis and research.

The number of countries from which statistics are available on a comparable, detailed basis, and at about the same time, is quite limited; actually, most are member countries of the OECD. But the OECD incorporates only about 15 percent of the number of countries in the UN, each of which is a market in which opportunities may be sought for exports. However, they are the most important trading nations. Therefore, the import statistics of over 100 countries were not available for use; they had to be, or could be, derived or constructed. This means that a total of imports of a product into a given foreign country, not itself reporting imports in the same detail or on the same timely basis, can be constructed by aggregating the exports to that country as reported by the principal trading nations of the world. They do not necessarily include the principal trading nations in any given product, but in any case, they would normally be the principal competition of U.S. exporters. Of course, if a given country reports its own import statistics on a timely basis they should be used. But if it does not, then its constructed, or derived, imports will serve the purpose.

The Matrix in Percentages

The technique involved in processing and presenting the data for practical business application is rather simple: construction of a matrix for international trade in a given product, with exporters listed on one axis, in a line across the top of the table, and with importers listed on the other, in a column at the left of the table. The statistics can be arranged in several ways, but for direct analytical usefulness, which is to ascertain percentage shares of markets for further study, Table 10 is a good model. It pertains to international trade in sewing machines and was developed from *Market Share Report* 70-90827. The report itself yields data on exports of the 14 principal exporting countries (Austria, Belgium-Luxembourg, Canada, Denmark, France, Germany, Italy, Japan, Netherlands, Norway, Sweden, Switzerland, United Kingdom, and the United States) to 90 foreign markets. Many of these countries of destination are small and the total number is not included in the table. Instead, only a few selected markets are used for illustrative purposes, listed as they appear in the basic report, which is not in alphabetic but in geographic arrangement.

Table 10. United States shares of exports of sewing machines from 14 supplier countries to the world and to selected destinations, 1968 (in percent of total import market).

Destination	*Total Exports from 14 Countries ($000)*	*United States*	*Japan*	*Germany*	*Italy*	*United Kingdom*	*Switzerland*	*Sweden*	*France*	*Netherlands*	*Other Reporting Countries*
World	$343,676	10	33	24	12	9	6	2	2	1	1
United States	93,107	—	59	11	12	13	3	2	*	na†	*
Canada	15,407	32	26	7	5	26	5	1	*	na	—
Brazil	4,851	25	27	34	7	4	1	*	*	na	3
Costa Rica	486	52	19	11	3	5	11	na	1	na	*
Ecuador	935	6	55	10	24	4	1	1	*	na	—
Mexico	5,162	43	16	18	12	10	*	na	*	na	—

Table 10 (Continued)

Destination	*Total Exports from 14 Countries ($000)*	*United States*	*Japan*	*Germany*	*Italy*	*United Kingdom*	*Switzerland*	*Sweden*	*France*	*Netherlands*	*Other Reporting Countries*
Venezuela	2,905	31	15	28	17	2	1	4	1	na	—
Belg./Lux.	7,709	11	11	27	13	2	15	2	2	16	°
France	23,332	7	6	56	13	6	10	°	—	2	1
Germany	21,238	13	35	—	16	10	7	2	5	9	4
Italy	13,452	9	1	76	—	5	3	°	1	3	1
Netherlands	10,408	12	19	45	9	2	5	4	1	na	3
United Kingdom	18,975	28	19	29	13	—	6	3	2	na	1
Denmark	3,427	6	22	32	8	6	14	9	1	na	1
Norway	3,738	4	1	23	8	3	20	40	°	na	2
Sweden	5,308	4	12	46	4	4	27	—	°	na	3
Austria	5,274	3	6	51	11	6	13	7	1	na	2
Switzerland	4,256	9	8	57	14	2	—	10	1	na	1
Ireland	2,044	10	27	17	3	43	1	°	°	na	—
Spain	3,516	11	2	49	20	9	5	°	2	na	3
Finland	3,005	4	1	31	18	9	11	24	°	na	2
USSR	3,356	1	24	18	48	1	°	na	9	na	—
Israel	1,527	17	28	31	11	2	7	na	2	na	1
Iran	3,382	1	49	21	15	7	5	1	1	na	1
Australia	9,203	13	33	13	6	15	18	2	1	na	°
So. Africa	6,663	15	25	19	16	8	11	1	5	na	°
Nigeria	988	1	29	12	30	14	°	°	12	na	°
Algeria	1,981	°	17	24	36	1	2	°	19	na	1
Japan	4,513	43	—	40	10	7	°	°	°	na	°
Malays/Sing.	2,289	3	74	7	5	10	1	°	°	na	—
Hong Kong	4,930	15	51	15	11	7	2	°	°	na	—
China (Taiwan)	4,044	2	91	2	3	°	2	na	na	na	—
Indonesia	1,102	1	97	1	na	1	°	na	na	na	—
Korea	3,312	5	89	4	1	na	1	°	na	na	°
Philippines	1,585	16	60	3	1	19	2	°	°	na	—
Thailand	2,685	2	72	16	1	15	°	na	na	na	°

SOURCE: U.S. Department of Commerce, *Market Share Report* 70-90827, Commodity Series.

° Less than 1%.
† Not avilable or none.

In the example used, the only dollar figure shown is that of the total *derived* imports into the market. Nothing more is needed because an approximation of any exporting country's monetary value of exports to a given destination, if that should be desired, can be determined by applying its percentage share to the total. If more exact data are desired, they can be obtained from other sources. In other words, the purpose here is not to report basic statistics, which are available elsewhere, but to provide readily and easily usable analytical data for a specified purpose.

Table 10 shows that U.S. exporters captured widely varying shares of the identified foreign import markets for sewing machines in 1968, ranging from less than 5 percent for some to over 25 percent for a few. The fact that U.S. exporters are supplying a given share, say 5 to 10 percent or more of several markets, is undeniable evidence that the U.S. producers are competitive. (This conclusion is subject to modification to the extent that an export may not be commercially competitive in origin but may derive, instead, from foreign aid or other preferred origin.) Attention is drawn to the relative position enjoyed by the United States in the several markets shown. For example, the United States supplied 31 percent of Venezuela's imports and 28 percent of the United Kingdom's, but only 6 percent of the imports of sewing machines of Ecuador, 7 percent of those of France, and 4 percent of those of Norway. Furthermore, some of the markets in which the U.S. share is low are the larger-volume ones, while those in which the U.S. share is high are of smaller volume and are relatively less important as world markets go.

Why these differentials? Is it that exporters from other countries have a preferred standing regarding tariffs or quotas; or is it that their proximity might yield some savings in transport costs, or provide easier travel and personal contacts or offer some language advantage or other intangible cultural "in" for reaching into the market? Or could it be that American direct investors are producing in that market or that some American companies that might be considered potential or probable exporters to a given foreign market have licensed the production in those markets to other, foreign producers?

It is possible to calculate this share position for, say, the last three or four years to determine whether there is any trend in the U.S. share or in that of other countries, or whether the size of the total import market may be increasing or decreasing. By comparing a company's own record with that of all U.S. exporters, its own progress or retrogression can be gauged as the basis for corrective action, if any is necessary.

The most readily available publication offering the most extensive data from which market share percentages can be developed is the series of reports mentioned earlier. The annual series covers the five preceding years and provides data on exports of 1,109 commodity groupings of manufactured products to 90 destinations. A single report costs only 10¢.

In each commodity report the totality of imports is derived from reported exports of 14 countries. Exports from the United States and from the eight leading foreign suppliers among the other 13 countries are listed in descending order, based on the value of each country's exports to the world of the commodity category in the last year of those included in the report.

In its present form, the report must be reduced to percentages for presenting data in the most easily comparable and useful form. There are, as explained in the technical notes accompanying each report, a number of qualifications to the data available through the reports as well as the shortcoming that the data reported cover trade only in certain manufactured products. (Unfortunately similar reports are not offered by the U.S. government for agricultural and mineral products.)

In summary, the typical uses of the *Market Share Reports* for private business are:

1. Determining a rank order of foreign import markets for the identifiable products in which a company may be interested, so the more important ones can receive first attention.
2. Ascertaining the strength and origin of foreign competition in each of the identified markets, and seeing whether such competition is increasing or decreasing.
3. Determining whether the U.S. share in any of the identified markets is increasing or decreasing.
4. Identifying those areas in which U.S. export activity is not saturated, and investigating them for developmental effort.
5. Identifying those areas in which American exporters are doing well, to ascertain whether more extensive market development effort is worthwhile.
6. Determining whether, for a company already exporting, its own share is increasing or decreasing relative to total U.S. performance. For example, if the U.S. share is increasing but a company's showing is contrary to the trend, it will be useful to the management to know this fact so corrective action can be taken.
7. Comparing, for U.S. companies manufacturing abroad and

selling from there to third countries, individual performance to the total for shippers from the country in which located, assuming it to be one of the reporting countries.

Limitations of International Trade Statistics

As great as have been improvements in recent years, international trade statistics are subject to a number of shortcomings insofar as a particular business is concerned. Among these are:

1. Statistical categories, either national or internationally agreed upon, are often too broad to be directly relatable to a firm's single product. Many U.S. export statistical categories, for example, include ten or more specific, identifiable items in the category and some include as many as 50 to 100. Internationally agreed-on categories are not as detailed as are statistics collected and reported by the United States and by certain other countries.

2. Parts and accessories are sometimes included in the same category as the finished product.

3. Classifications used by the United States for exports and imports are not always identical.

4. Figures are necessarily historical and may not be as current as one would like. Furthermore, they cannot give adequate intelligence on some new products that formerly were included in a mixed group because they were relatively unimportant at that time in international trade.

5. Not all reports are published at the same time, nor are they otherwise available at the same time. Some become available only a year or more after comparable figures from another country.

6. When the import statistics are derived from export statistics of reporting countries, shipments to certain destinations may not necessarily reflect the ultimate destination of the merchandise. This fact may be significant in trade and transshipment centers, including Hong Kong and certain countries of northern Europe, such as Belgium, The Netherlands, and Germany, through whose ports shipments for inland European countries are routed.

7. In the statistics available through international organizations, and especially for those whose most effective use is on a comparative basis, there are certain gaps such as exclusions of data (usually mentioned in the accompanying technical notes) and the nonavailability of data from one or more countries for certain products.

8

Foreign Market Development

Identifying foreign market opportunities, as discussed so far, is like identifying an area in which to go fishing or hunting. One does not just appear with a fishing rod or gun. He must find a precise spot, he may need a guide (at least for best results), and he must have the right equipment to attract or to reach his objective.

What can be accomplished through procedures covered in the preceding chapter is not the identification of an export opportunity but of where an opportunity appears to be. This is primarily the selection of a country or countries in which further effort and expense seem justified—in effect, zeroing in on what appear to be the more promising of possible opportunities. Additional, specific information is needed in order to determine whether the apparent market is worth entering or developing. What is sought is internal rather than comparative intelligence, and it must be of various dimensions—economic, commercial, political, cultural, social, and possibly others. The type of intelligence needed is institutional and structural rather than theoretical.

FOREIGN MARKET SURVEYS

We are moving here into foreign market surveys, an aspect of market research, the basics of which for this purpose encompass inquiry into such points as: (1) population and its characteristics; (2) freedom of those in the market to buy in open competition, for example, the use of exchange controls or import licensing; (3) the distribution system for the product; (4) the nature and position of other foreign competition, for example, tariff preferences or long-established contacts; and (5) consumer attitudes and demands.

Who does this research, and his objectives, will determine the information sought; and the information sought may be instrumental in dictating who does the research. It may be a government or a trade association, or a private company doing the investigation for itself or under contract for someone else. In any case, one must eventually concern himself with, if not start with, a product or product type.

In the reduction of more than 100 countries to a very few for detailed investigation, it has already been shown that general, imprecise knowledge can serve to delineate some markets. But to be more factual, more detailed analysis is required. However, the collection and study of detailed data can be justified only when the field has already been somewhat narrowed down because a company could not afford to go through the process for 125 or 130 countries when looking for only a few.

Basic Statistical Indicators

The reduction of many countries to a few can be facilitated by reference to a very few easily available statistical indicators and to certain supplemental statistical data. Consider population, overall trade with the United States, and geographic size. What does population indicate about markets that deserve further detailed investigation? Alone, not much. For example, the population of Kuwait is 325,000; that of India is 453,000,000—a relationship of 1 to almost 1,100. But U.S. exports to Kuwait in 1969 were $109 million, while to India they were $717 million—a relationship of one to seven. Or compare Japan and India. Their population relationship is one to five, but U.S. exports to Japan are almost seven times as large as those to India.

Again, considering population alone, 18 of 33 countries in Asia and Oceania have populations of more than 5 million each. So have 7 in Latin America, 13 in Europe, and 14 in Africa. Population information obviously is not enough. Other characteristics are significant, for example, area. Some countries possess less than 10,000 square miles, while several large ones exceed 3 million:

USSR	8,649,000
China	3,692,000
Canada	3,852,000
U.S.	3,628,000
Brazil	2,386,000

This, then, resolves into population density, but for our purpose it still tells little, or practically nothing.

Other Factors

Other general factors pertaining to a country must be studied if they bear on the desirability or use of a given product. These factors include:

- Stage of economic development
- Age grouping
- Per capita income
- Urbanization (population of major cities)
- Educational level, or literacy
- Communications media (newspapers, radio and TV, theaters, telephones)
- Transportation network
- Construction activity (residential and other)
- Gross national product (total, by origin, and per capita)
- Direction, volume, and structure of foreign trade
- Price indices
- Monetary reserves and foreign exchange rates

Not all the foregoing bear on every foreign market for every product, and many other indicators could be of use in market research, but there must be a basis for their applicability to the given situation and, above all, the intelligence must be available. This is a serious problem, even in many advanced countries.

The Wall Street Journal of February 12, 1968, reported that European countries are moving to improve their collection and availability of economic data, considered in some cases to be too slow and too little. Among the shortcomings cited in the article are the differences in the way statistics are reported by different countries, and their lack of timeliness in collection and frequency in reporting statistics.

Nonstatistical Factors

In addition to voluminous statistical data, certain intangibles must be considered. These include stability of the government and structural and institutional factors, such as internal marketing practices and distribution channels. Moreover, the accessibility to or the environmental atmosphere of a foreign market must be studied to appraise its developmental prospects. The factors pertaining to accessibility and what can be called atmospheric characteristics are descriptive rather than statistical, and can be considered legalistic to some extent. They differ, of course, from country to country and can best be learned by observation and by reference to a variety of economic and political papers and documents. These are, furthermore, the types of intelligence that pertain not only to original entry but to a company's continuing export possibility and effort in a given market.

Continuous Marketing Intelligence

Both statistical and nonstatistical factors can mesh into what becomes, or could become, an instrument for continuous market development—an extension and a refinement of the information sought and analyzed before entering a given market. The evolution of the idea, and the advantages of a continuous marketing information system, are interestingly presented in an article in *Business Management.*[1]

Much of the information desired for and useful in market cultivation and development is available from secondary sources, and much of the research necessary can be conducted by home-based personnel. This relates to such broad factors as overall economic

---

[1] "Marketing Intelligence Systems—A DEW (Distant Early Warning) Line for Marketing Men," *Business Management,* January 1966.

conditions, amount of existing imports and their sources, rate of growth of imports, and relative ease of access to a country. Some of the refinements and more precise analyses and applications can better, and perhaps only, be accomplished abroad, from primary sources. But before spending much time and money on the market research itself, *market access* must be evaluated for any market that appears deserving of detailed investigation. This covers points such as geographic proximity, transportation availability, foreign trade regulations, special trading relationships, quantitative limitations on sourcing of imports, and currency convertibility.

Foreign market development includes, then, two major segments: identification and investigation of a market prior to entry (its attractiveness and apparent potential), and its intensive development once in; and this can only be done through direct exporting.

At this point the earlier reference to a guide on a hunting or fishing expedition comes to mind. Eventually, the guide may be one's own sales subsidiary, with hired employees. But more probably, and at least in the beginning, the direct link with the foreign market will be an agent or distributor on the spot who is already familiar with the market and its practices and problems. This seems to be the way most companies penetrate a foreign market, by having someone in the foreign country working in the exporter's interest. Whether he is paid a salary or a commission is not important; what is important is that he be a recognized and dependable link in the exporter's distribution system.

FOREIGN REPRESENTATIVES

Because one's representative abroad is usually an independent businessman (or sometimes a firm) and is given exclusive and protected sales rights within a delineated area (ordinarily a region or country) for the named product or products, an exporter must rely heavily on the representation. Therefore, not only must a representative be carefully selected; the contract with him must be thorough and should anticipate and provide for the handling of unpleasant situations before they become real problems.

An exporter wants to be sure of a foreign representative's ability to sell and his willingness to put forth good effort, but he also wants assurance about a potential representative's personal and professional attributes: business background and references, reputation, organization and personnel, finances, lines already handled, and demonstrated ability. In this connection banks are of considerable assistance, as are credit reporting agencies such as Dun & Bradstreet, Inc., whose international services are very extensive.

Similarly, a representative abroad expects something of the exporter. First, a responsible business connection abroad will want to know as much about us as we want to know about him. Second, there is no more reason for him to be interested in taking on a new line, ours, and possibly cutting down on his old ones, than there is for a domestic firm to do so. Moreover, he will probably have a hard time introducing a product if it is new and not well known. Because his only reason for dealing with us is profit, there must be enough potential gain involved to make it worthwhile for him. Perhaps our product may be only a small share of his total business, or it may be the biggest share. The important point is that it must be big enough to call forth his best effort. He, too, makes his profit from the last increments of sales, so it is necessary to determine the potential and to work with him to develop and achieve it for mutual benefit. Moreover, when he is encouraged to work on our product he does so rather than concentrating on others.

A representative, especially an agent, is tied in to the exporter by contract and by provisions in commercial law that vary from country to country and that in some respects cannot be contracted away. Therefore an agency arrangement in some countries carries with it rights and obligations of more than passing significance to the exporter. The legal requirements are, after all, designed to protect the individual or firm in the foreign country and not primarily the exporter who appoints the agent. The importance of foreign laws in international agency arrangements is exceptionally well covered in an article published by the International Trade Centre of GATT.[2]

Principal Elements of an Agency Contract

Having someone abroad responsibly tied in to a company's export effort is a necessity as much as it is an advantage. And because of the operational and legal aspects of agency relationships, he must be carefully selected; one cannot change such appointments arbitrarily. The time to do the investigating is before the marriage, not after. The working relationship must be spelled out

---

[2] Giberga, Ovidio M., "Foreign Laws Can Bind Your Agency Agreement," *International Trade Forum,* December 1968.

in contractual details, covering those points that give both principal and agent the assurances they desire. Many articles have been written on the form and content of such an agreement but it should be obvious that, aside from a few fundamental and general points, the many details must be tailored to fit the case.

Following is a list of the principal points to be considered in drawing up an agency contract once the company is satisfied about the attributes a representative should have: demonstrated ability to sell, number of salesmen or size of organization, territory in which active, other accounts handled, financial condition and reputation, contacts in the area, technical competence, political connections, and so on.

1. Clarity as to legal status and capacity of agent to contract (firm, partnership, corporation).
2. Authenticity of language and text of content, should difficulties as to interpretation arise.
3. Dates of coming into force and normal expiration of contract, that is, date, in case of fixed time period, or conditions under which contract shall cease.
4. Contractual products.
5. Contractual territory.
6. Contractual clientele, that is, groups of customers to be or not to be canvassed by agent.
7. Nature of exclusive agency rights, that is, degree of exclusivity, particularly sole agent's rights in respect of orders placed directly with principal.
8. Rights and obligations of principal:
    a. Acceptance of orders, that is, whether orders shall be subject to acceptance by the principal and, if so, whether reason for not accepting need be given to agent.
    b. Information to agent about production and sales program and policy.
    c. Manufacturing or licensing in contractual territory.
    d. Protection of sole and exclusive rights of agent.
    e. Unfair competition (undertaking of legal steps to protect against patent infringement, trademark usage, and so on, but with agent obligated to bring infringements to attention of principal.
    f. Sales aids, advertising matter, and payment of cost of publicity and of customs and other charges on advertising material.
    g. Traveling and other expenses.

9. Rights and obligations of agent:
   a. Good and serious performance; protecting rights and interest of principal; maintenance of separate banking account for funds received for principal.
   b. Power to enter into binding agreements on behalf of principal, either through the contract or by operation of law in the representative's country.
   c. Capacity to act in name of principal.
   d. Observance of conditions of sale (prices, delivery time, payment, and so on), that is, extent to which law of the contractual territory allows the agent to be bound by instructions of principal.
   e. Prohibition of competitive activities, extending into period following expiration or termination of contract.
   f. Right to purchase for own account.
   g. Consignment stocks, that is, insurance of such stocks and conditions under which they are to be or may be returned.
   h. Service after sale and spare parts.
   i. Provision of commercial and financial information.
   j. Arrangement and organization of sales work (control over subagents).
   k. Insolvent customers, that is, agent's responsibility to assure himself as to solvency of customers whose orders he transmits to the principal.
   l. Protection of, or notification to principal of, violation of his industrial property rights.
   m. Collection of sums due, in cases in which customers do not pay directly to principal.
   n. *Del credere* arrangements, such as amount of guarantee and extent of agent's liability under each guarantee.
   o. Minimum sales (impact of nonacceptance of orders by principal, failure to deliver, imposition of import restrictions, and so on).
   p. Guaranteed minimum income.
   q. Right to assign contract.

10. Commission (basis net or gross invoice; items to be deducted, if net):
    a. Sales by others within protected territory; sales by agent in other territories.
    b. When commission accrues and when payable; when order transmitted or accepted; when goods shipped; when paid.

c. Effect on commission of subsequent events (cancellation of order, bankruptcy of buyer, reduction in price, and so on).
d. Commission on repeat orders perhaps not solicited by agent.

11. Expiration of contract or conditions for earlier termination:
a. Effects to survive termination (unfilled outstanding orders).
b. Preservation of trade secrets for stated period.
c. Abstention from acts of competition for stated period.
d. Compensation of agent for termination of contract by principal for other than wrongful act by agent.

12. Conflict of laws and competent jurisdiction.

The items in this list were extracted from the International Chamber of Commerce booklet, "Commercial Agency—Guide for the Drawing Up of Contracts Between Parties Residing in Different Countries."[3] The booklet also points out that when negotiating a contract, the parties should ascertain the exact position of legal interpretation, the incidence of customs and usages of the particular trade, the conflict of laws, and the economic problems that may pertain in a given situation.

FINDING AND SELECTING A REPRESENTATIVE

Of one thing we can be fairly certain: good representatives are hard to find, and usually are already spoken for. Selection of a good agent or distributor provides the chance to develop the market aggressively. As one writer said, one should choose the best agent available and then by judicious handling make him into a good one.[4]

Where does one find information about representatives abroad (something quite apart from economic conditions in the country, distribution channels, and the like)? As in any sizable city or area of the United States, where one is likely to find several people in the same line of business more or less competing with each other, so it is abroad in most places. So we can picture the

---

[3] Publication 213, International Chamber of Commerce, 38 Cours Albert 1er, Paris 8, France.

[4] G. W. Marshall, "Appointing a Good Agent," *Board of Trade Journal*, March 12, 1965, p. 547.

problem by asking how, in a country like England, Japan, or Argentina, one can confidently and with minimum expense narrow down the entire business and industry segment to *one* company, and perhaps to one man.

Many trade associations, chambers of commerce, transportation companies, or port promotional agencies publicize export and agency opportunities. The trouble is that they give very little, if any, background information on the companies they list. Yet the fact is that while one is looking for a potential distributor, many distributors are also looking for potential suppliers.

Frequently leads acquired from such facilities do not give the name of the prospect abroad; instead, a code number may be used and one must write to the association or company for details. A good example of this is *Worldwide Marketing Opportunities*, published by Pan American World Airways. The January 1971 issue contained seven pages of worldwide marketing opportunities. Figure 5 shows the first page of that listing.

Opportunities Publicized in Commerce Today

Every second week, the U.S. Department of Commerce publishes in *Commerce Today* a section called "Foreign Trade Opportunities," which lists the names of foreign firms interested either in direct purchase or sale relationships with U.S. business firms, or in agency arrangements. They are listed by product and by country. Figure 6 shows the first part of that section. Every country of any commercial significance performs the service of aiding its exporters or potential exporters with commercial intelligence. In the United States this is the job primarily of the Foreign Service. Intelligence is gathered by commercial attachés, screened or evaluated, and sent to the Department of Commerce, which passes it on to the business community. The department also picks up names of potential prospects uncovered by trade missions.

Commercial intelligence provided by the government is emphasized because it is the most extensive in coverage and probably the most complete of such services. Much of it is free to the recipient, but its costs are substantial and not many private companies could perform the function except as a matter of publicity, which itself is a cost that must be budgeted and financed. In the case of U.S. commercial intelligence, not only is it possible to get leads by name, but one is assured that back-up information on the name is also available. Back-up is in the form of data contained in a *World Trade Directory Report,* as shown in Figure 7.

FIGURE 5.

Partial list of worldwide marketing opportunities.

Worldwide Marketing Opportunities

Buyers and sellers around the world are offered these free listings each month by Pan American. For names and addresses of listed firms, write on your letterhead to Manager-Marketing Services, Pan American World Airways, Pan Am Building, New York, N.Y. 10017. Be sure to include coded number which precedes each listing. To help Pan Am provide a quality service for all concerned, please type inquiries and limit them to not more than 20 items of genuine interest to your business.

ANDORRA

H-1: **REPRODUCTIONS** of famous oil paintings, antiques, etc.—firm seeks contacts, buyers worldwide.

H-2: **GENERAL MERCHANDISE**—firm seeks importers worldwide.

AUSTRIA

H-3: **ADVERTISING GIFTS,** promotion articles, mail order items—importer seeks manufacturers, suppliers worldwide.

H-4: **OIL PAINTINGS,** original—exporter seeks buyers worldwide.

H-5: **FOAM RUBBER** parts for shoes—manufacturer seeks contacts with shoemakers worldwide.

H-6: **TROPICAL FISH** and plants — importer seeks suppliers worldwide.

H-7: **MACHINERY,** electronic, automatic to produce ceiling girders for building industry; also machinery to make spikes for tires—firm seeks producers, buyers, licensees worldwide.

BELGIUM

H-8: **MERRY-GO-ROUND** motorcycles and accessories—manufacturer seeks buyers, agents worldwide.

H-9: **SOAPS,** detergents—manufacturer seeks to export worldwide.

H-10: **AIR TUBE CONVEYORS**—manufacturer seeks distributors worldwide except United Kingdom, Holland, Sweden, Spain, Portugal, Italy.

DENMARK

H-11: **GARDEN TILLERS** and 2-wheel tractors — manufacturer seeks importers worldwide.

H-12: **LIVESTOCK FEED** or supplement, also pet food—manufacturer and distributor seeks agency for, or license to produce, brand-name line.

H-13: **BADMINTON** rackets and equipment—firm seeks to import from Japan, Indonesia, Malaysia.

ENGLAND

H-14: **DESK PAD,** novelty, world patents pending—manufacturer seeks distributors worldwide.

H-15: **FORK LIFT TRUCKS,** industrial tractors, platform trucks, mechanical handling equipment — manufacturer seeks buyers worldwide.

H-16: **TWEED NECKTIES**—firm seeks to export worldwide.

H-17: **SAUSAGE CASINGS,** edible—importer seeks contacts with manufacturers worldwide.

H-18: **LANCASHIRE CLOGS,** children's sizes—manufacturer seeks distributors in U.S.A.

H-19: **LIFEJACKETS** and bouyancy aids—manufacturer seeks markets worldwide.

H-20: **ANTIQUES** and oil paintings—firm seeks buyers U.S.A. and Canada.

H-21: **POSTAGE STAMP** packets, topical, country — firm seeks buyers, distributors worldwide.

H-22: **WHISKEY,** liqueurs, German wines—firm seeks agents worldwide.

H-23: **EXERCISE** equipment, rowing machines, chest expanders, speed toboggan, etc. — manufacturer seeks sales worldwide.

H-24: **PRINTS,** hand colored, from antique plates; classical, military and sporting — firm seeks retail or mail order markets worldwide.

H-25: **SOAP DISPENSERS,** liquid — hand soap manufacturer seeks suppliers of dispensers.

H-26: **GASOLINE ENGINES,** vertical crankshaft, fractional to multiple horsepower — firm seeks manufacturers, suppliers worldwide.

H-27: **SWEATERS,** British Shetland, child and adult sizes — firm seeks importers, wholesalers worldwide.

H-28: **LEISURE EQUIPMENT,** saddlery, tents, camping accessories, trailers, clothing — distributor seeks suppliers worldwide.

H-29: **BOOMERANGS,** wooden, decorative—manufacturer seeks buyers, distributors worldwide.

H-30: **PRINTS,** hand screen, of British historical buildings and churches, sizes up to 30 x 40 inches—exporter seeks outlets in U.S.A.

H-31: **BURGLAR** and fire alarms, accessories; also radios, portable multiband including very high frequency bands for aircraft, shipping, police, etc.—importer seeks suppliers worldwide.

H-32: **MAIL ORDER** lines, new products and ideas—firm seeks to import worldwide.

H-33: **DOG COATS,** imitation fur lined, also leather covered steering wheels and consols—firm seeks distributors in U.S.A., Japan, Australia.

H-34: **PET DOORS**—manufacturer seeks markets worldwide.

H-35: **AEROSOL** non-stick surface spray for saucepans and oven glassware—manufacturer seeks agents, importers worldwide.

H-36: **USED TRACTOR PARTS,** second hand motor vehicles and spares—dealer seeks buyers worldwide.

H-37: **GLASS** cullets, scrap, washed and unwashed, regular and large quantities—supplier seeks buyers worldwide.

H-38: **FURNITURE** for garden and patio, flower pedestals, stands; made of wrought iron, parana pine—firm seeks importers, distributors in U.S.A., Caribbean, Australia.

H-39: **DENTURE** repair kit, personal — manufacturer seeks customers worldwide.

H-40: **POTTERY** tankards, pomanders, toby jugs, tableware, mail order items—manufacturer seeks outlets in U.S.A.

H-41: **WIGS,** human and synthetic hair — firm seeks distributors worldwide.

H-42: **SHOCK STICKS,** electronic; anti-riot equipment, security devices for police and military — manufacturer seeks contacts worldwide.

H-269: **KANGAROO** skin coats, rugs, chamois, sheepskins — agent seeks buyers worldwide.

H-270: **MARINE EQUIPMENT,** hand tools, injection syringes, construction appliances, plywood, natural rubber, bulbs for car lamps, insulating tapes, steel chains, building materials —importer seeks to represent manufacturers.

H-271: **AUDIO EQUIPMENT,** tape recorders, etc., and domestic anti-pollution equipment—firm seeks to import worldwide.

H-272: **INDUSTRIAL RAW MATERIALS,** chemicals, electrical components, sunglasses, optics, electronic watches and veterinary x-ray equipment — firm seeks suppliers worldwide. Also seeks markets or distributors for television productions, documentaries, etc., in U.S.A., Canada, England and Europe.

H-273: **FROZEN SHARK,** heads and livers—firm seeks buyers worldwide.

H-274: **NAIL PLATE** timber connectors, non-weld girder clamps, manufacturer seeks to export, license joint ventures worldwide; also seeks to import, export or manufacture under license builders hardware.

H-275: **POSTERS,** pop art—firm seeks to import, export worldwide.

H-276: **PLAN-PRINTING** machines, developing machines and plan trimmer—manufacturer seeks agents, distributors worldwide except Taiwan and Malaysia; also seeks to import or acquire agencies for fractional horsepower DC electric motors and drawing office instruments.

H-277: **GRANDMOTHER CLOCKS,** 4/4 Westminster chime, also grandfather clocks and movements—firm seeks to import from Europe; also seeks to act as general import/export agent for New Zealand.

H-278: **ELECTRIC SLICING KNIVES,** battery powered, for domestic use—firm seeks to import worldwide.

H-279: **CAR TRAILERS,** half-ton, letterboxes, wheelbarrows, also decorative pistol and bronze shield wall placques—supplier seeks outlets Pacific area.

ALGERIA

H-283: **SHRIMP,** wine, handicrafts, early vegetables and fruit — firm seeks to export worldwide. Also to represent manufacturers of industrial, aircraft, handling equipment.

H-284: **EXOTIC PRODUCTS,** hardware, hosiery, cosmetics, building materials, etc. — firm seeks to import/export worldwide.

CAMEROON

H-285: **CLOTHING,** readymade, textiles—firm seeks representatives in European Economic Community.

H-286: **AFRICAN GIFT** items, smokers articles, masks, religious articles, etc.—firm seeks buyers, markets worldwide.

CONGO

H-287: **MINERALS**—firm seeks contacts in Germany, Italy, Israel, Switzerland, Asia.

DAHOMEY

H-288: **ELECTRIC TORCHES,** enameled articles, razor blades —firm seeks to import worldwide.

GHANA

H-289: **TIMBER LOGS,** foodstuffs, handicrafts, etc. — exporter seeks contacts worldwide.

H-290: **WEST AFRICAN GRAY PARROTS,** small animals—exporter seeks contacts worldwide.

IVORY COAST

H-291: **ART,** West African negro; carved ivories, curious jewelry —exporter seeks markets in U.S.A. and Canada.

H-292: **NATIVE HANDICRAFTS,** garment decorations, tortoise sheils, fabrics—firm seeks customers worldwide.

MOROCCO

H-293: **CALICO,** unbleached — manufacturer wishes to export worldwide.

H-294: **NOVELTY** and gift items, advertising gadgets — importer seeks manufacturers, suppliers worldwide.

NIGERIA

H-295: **GARMENTS,** readymade, flash lights, kerosene stoves, wall and table clocks, watches, watchbands, belts, cutlery, bicycle parts and accessories, office stationery, toys — firm seeks suppliers worldwide.

H-296: **ART,** traditional and contemporary, crafts, masks, carvings, bronze and leather work, knick-knacks, etc.—firm seeks buyers worldwide.

H-297: **SUNGLASSES,** mirror glasses, clothing, kerosene stoves, and wicks, cutlery, jewelry, clocks, wristwatches and bands, patent medicines—firm seeks suppliers worldwide.

SOUTH AFRICA

H-298: **TEXTILES,** textile machinery, timber, paper, chemicals — agent seeks suppliers worldwide.

H-299: **FIBERGLASS** mouldings, door facings, shutters, pilasters, pediments and decorative wall plaques — manufacturer seeks to export worldwide.

H-300: **PRINTERS BLANK CARDS,** fancy invitation, wedding, gilded, etc. — manufacturer seeks wholesalers in U.S.A., Canada, Australia, Europe.

TANZANIA

H-301: **TEXTILES** and garments of local design, shirts, socks, etc.—manufacturer seeks markets worldwide.

TUNISIA

H-302: **JEANS, SLACKS, SHORTS** and work clothes — apparel maker uses customers' own materials, seeks clients worldwide.

H-303: **SALT,** low priced, large quantity—exporter seeks distributors, buyers worldwide.

H-304: **OIL PAINTINGS.** water colors, engravings, acrylic paintings — painter wishes to export to U.S.A. and Canada.

EL SALVADOR

H-305: **FRESH LIMES,** U.S.D.A. approved, medium/large, available through March—producer seeks buyers in Europe and U.S.A.

GUATEMALA

H-306: **GOLD** and silver jewelry with Mayan gods, medallions, cufflinks, tie clips, bracelets, etc. for mail order—firm seeks buyer and agents in U.S.A. and West Germany.

ARGENTINA

H-307: **SHOES,** ladies', childrens' and mens' — manufacturer wishes to export worldwide.

H-308: **LEATHER WATCH BANDS** for wristwatches—firm seeks buyers from U.S.A. and Europe.

H-309: **ROSE PLANTS,** pocket size on order, other plants, bulbs, seeds, flowers, etc.—firm seeks buyer and agents worldwide.

H-310: **ABA RESAI** packed in giant cactus cases, dry liquor, grape seed oil, indian tonic — manufacturer seeks to export worldwide.

13

FIGURE 6.
Partial list of foreign trade opportunities.

Foreign Trade Opportunities

These trade opportunities are based on reports received from the U.S. Foreign Service by the International Liaison and Trade Opportunities Staff and other units of the Bureau of Domestic Commerce (BDC), U.S. Department of Commerce, Washington, D.C. 20230. The commodities in which foreign firms are interested are indicated by the five-digit numbers and commodity classifications which are from the Standard Industrial Classification (SIC) Manual and the Numerical List of Manufactured Products, 1967 Census of Manufacturers used extensively by Government and industry.

U.S. firms should also be aware that the listing in *Commerce Today* of opportunities to trade in specific commodities and technical data does not necessarily imply approval of their export by the Department of Commerce pursuant to the Export Administration Act of 1969. Applicable export licensing regulations must be followed.

Every effort is made to include only firms or individuals with good reputations. However, the Department cannot be responsible for any trade relations.

The mark (•) indicates that this trade opportunity is a request for bids by a foreign government agency. A (★) at the end means that additional information may be borrowed by U.S. firms from the individual division of BDC. To avoid delays, requests for loan material should specify the country, commodity and foreign government agency.

WTD indicates that a World Trade Directory Report containing financial and business background information on the foreign firm is available for $2 from the U.S. Department of Commerce, BIC-924, Washington, D.C. 20230 or from any Commerce Field Office.

Agencies

Specific foreign firms have expressed interest in agency agreements for the products listed below. Exclusive agencies for these products are wanted only if specified.

Dairy products

20221 — SWEDEN — Cheese, mozzarella. Hermansson Restaurant AB (importer, restaurants on franchising basis), 8 C Torsgatan, S-752 22 Uppsala. WTD 10/70.

Canning, preserving foods

20331—GERMANY—Canned fruits. Correspondence requested in German. Kuehlhallen und Eisfabrik Dr. Karl Lieblich & Co. KG. (storage facility), 42-50 Krailenshaldenstrasse, D-7000 Stuttgart 30, Baden-Wuerttemberg. WTD 9/70.

20332—GERMANY—Canned vegetables. Correspondence requested in German. Kuehlhallen und Eisfabrik Dr. Karl Lieblich & Co. KG. (storage facility), 42-50 Krailenshaldenstrasse, D-7000 Stuttgart 30, Baden-Wuerttemberg. WTD 9/70.

20336—SWEDEN—Pizza sauces, frozen. Hermansson Restaurant AB (importer, restaurants on franchising basis), 8 C Torsgatan, S-752 22 Uppsala. WTD 10/70.

20372—GERMANY—Frozen vegetables. Correspondence requested in German. Kuehlhallen und Eisfabrik Dr. Karl Lieblich & Co. KG. (storage facility), 42-50 Krailenshaldenstrasse, D-7000 Stuttgart 30, Baden-Wuerttemberg, WTD 9/70.

20373 — GERMANY — Frozen prepared foods. Correspondence requested in German. Kuehlhallen und Eisfabrik Dr. Karl Lieblich & Co. KG. (storage facility), 42-50 Krailenshaldenstrasse, D-7000 Stuttgart 30, Baden-Wuerttemberg. WTD 9/70.

20373 — SWEDEN — Frozen pizza pies. Hermansson Restaurant AB (importer, restaurants on franchising basis), 8 C Torsgatan, S-752 22 Uppsala. WTD 10/70.

Broad woven fabric mills, cotton

22110 — LEBANON — Cotton fabrics. Shaker Hallak & Sons (importer, agent), Maktaby & Bank Zalkha Bldg., Allenby St., P.O. Box 3100, Beirut. WTD 11/70.

Broad woven fabric mills, manmade fiber, silk

22210 — LEBANON — Synthetic fabrics. Shaker Hallak & Sons (importer, agent), Maktaby & Bank Zalkha Bldg., Allenby St., P.O. Box 3100, Beirut. WTD 11/70.

22212—VIET-NAM—Tropical weight fabrics for men, women's clothing; finished textiles suitable for drapes, curtains. K. A. J. Chotirmall & Cie. (importer, dist., agent), 34-36 Phan Boi Chau, Saigon. WTD 11/70.

22212—VIET-NAM—Tropical weight fabrics for men, women's clothing; finished textiles suitable for drapes, curtains. Comptoir Indien (importer, dist., agent), 142 Le Thanh Ton, Saigon. WTD in prep.

22218 — AUSTRALIA—Terylene fabrics suitable for making window curtains. Sanderson & Cork (importer, dist., agent), Commerce House, 328 Flinders St., Melbourne 3000. WTD 10/69.

Broad woven fabric mills, wool

22310—LEBANON—Wool fabrics. Shaker Hallak & Sons (importer, agent), Maktaby & Bank Zalkha Bldg., Allenby St., P.O. Box 3100, Beirut. WTD 11/70.

Floor covering mills, products

22720—SWITZERLAND—Tufted, printed wall-to-wall carpets, all kinds. Rolf Bumbach AG; Attn: Mr. Bumbach (dist., agent), Hardstrasse 9, P.O. Box 8040 Zurich. WTD in prep.

Textile goods

22992 — AUSTRALIA — Printed linen furnishing fabrics. Sanderson & Cork (importer, dist., agent), Commerce House, 328 Flinders St., Melbourne 3000. WTD 10/69.

Men's coats

23100—Men's cotton coats, 7,200 in large sizes. Available for export not for sale because purchased as foreign surplus property of U.S. Government. Now held in bond on West Coast by J. M. Siegel, 465 E. Third St., Los Angeles, Calif. 90013.

Paper mills, products

26211—ISRAEL—Newsprint. Agency for Israel, Cyprus. G. & G. Foreign Trade Co. Ltd. (importer, agent, exporter), Shalom Tower, 9 Ahad Ha'am St., (P.O. Box 29239), Tel Aviv. WTD 7/69.

Converted paper products

26472—ISRAEL—Facial, cleansing tissues, toilet paper, etc. Agency for Israel, Cyprus. G. & G. Foreign Trade Co. Ltd. (importer, agent, exporter), Shalom Tower, 9 Ahad Ha'am St., (P.O. Box 29239), Tel Aviv. WTD 7/69.

Industrial chemicals

28160—ITALY—Oxides for manufacture of enamels for ceramic industry. Rey di Gavioli Rag. Gastone (importer, agent, exporter), 40 Corso Cavour, I 41100-Modena. WTD 11/70.

28181—TAIWAN—Dye intermediates, etc. Lynnbros Industrial Co., Ltd. (importer, agent), 7, Lane 118, Chien Kou North Rd., Taipei. WTD 9/70.

28199—TAIWAN—Other inorganic chemicals. Lynnbros Industrial Co., Ltd. (importer, agent), 7, Lane 118, Chien Kou North Rd., Taipei. WTD 9/70.

Synthetic materials

28220 — ISRAEL — Polyisoprene to replace natural rubber. M. Dothan Ltd. (importer, dist., agent), P.O. Box 1995, Tel Aviv. WTD in prep.

28230—LEBANON—Cellulosic manmade fibers. Shaker Hallak & Sons (importer, agent), Maktaby & Bank Zalkha Bldg., Allenby St., P.O. Box 3100, Beirut. WTD 11/70.

FIGURE 7.
Sample of world trade directory report.

FORM 1A-341
9-70

☒ New ☐ Rev

WORLD TRADE DIRECTORY REPORT

U. S. DEPARTMENT OF COMMERCE
BUREAU OF INTERNATIONAL COMMERCE

PAGE 1 OF 3

Voluntary______ Trade or Investment Op______ Requested X (Form 1A-217 attached)

This report, submitted by the American Foreign Service, under the direction of the Secretary of State, is transmitted in confidence. No responsibility can be assumed by the Government or its officers for any transactions had with any persons or firms herein mentioned. The report is not for publication. All correspondence relating to information in this report should be conducted with the Commercial Intelligence Division, U.S. Department of Commerce, Washington, D.C. 20230. SECONDARY DISTRIBUTION PROHIBITED.

1. Country name: CANADA
2. Country code: 1 2 2 (1 2 3)
3. Serial number: 1 3 4 4 5 6 0 (4 5 6 7 8 9 10)

4. Firm name: SMITH, George M. and Sons (11-70)

5. Street address and P.O. Box No.: 124 Ermou Street (11-70)

6. City and State or Prov.: Toronto, Ontario (11-30)
6a. Country: Canada (31-38)

7. Type of organization (Check one): Proprietorship ☐ 39; Corporation ☒ 40; Partnership ☐ 41; Other ☐ 42 (See item 28)

8. Year established: 1920 (43 - 45)
9. Number of salesmen: 2 (46 - 52)
10. U.S. Rep.? (See item 26a) Yes ☒ 53; No ☐ 54

11. Working capital (Local currency): 3,394,110 (55 - 66)
12. Sales volume (Local currency): 56,726,655 (67 - 78)

13. Number of employees: 35 (11 - 17)
14. Relative size (Check one): Very large ☒ 18; Large ☐ 19; Medium ☐ 20; Small ☐ 21 (As regarded in country)

15. Is reputation of firm satisfactory? (See also Item 29) Yes ☒ 22; No ☐ 23

16. Purchase and Sales Areas *(Check appropriate blocks)*

	Purchase	Sales
Own Country	(24)	X (25)
United States	X (26)	(27)
Canada	(28)	(29)
Mexico, Central Am., Carib.	(30)	(31)
South America	(32)	(33)
Australia, Oceania	(34)	(35)
EFTA countries	X (36)	(37)
European common market	(38)	(39)
Other Europe	(40)	(41)
Southern Asia	(42)	(43)
Eastern Asia	(44)	(45)
Near East	(46)	(47)
Africa	(48)	(49)

17. Acceptable Language of Correspondence *(Check appropriate blocks)*

Native ☒ 50; English ☐ 51; French ☐ 52; German ☐ 53; Spanish ☐ 54; Portuguese ☐ 55; Italian ☐ 56; Arabic ☐ 57

18. Date of information: Month 1 0 (58 59); Year 7 0 (60 61) *(Last two digits)*

☆ U.S. GOVERNMENT PRINTING OFFICE: 1970—405-002

FIGURE 7.

(Continued).

PAGE 2 OF 3

WTD on SMITH, George M. and Sons, Toronto, Ontario, Canada
Name and address

19. Product Description, SIC and Business Codes - Up to 15 different products can be listed below; for each product enter the product name, SIC code, and up to five business codes. The business codes to be used are as follows:

0 Manufacturer
1 Retailer
2 Agent (sales or indent)
3 Distributor (incl. wholesale)
4 Exporter
5 Importer
6 Cooperative
7 Engineering
8 Construction
9 Other *(Specify in Item 28)*

	Description of Product	SIC Code	Business Codes
A.	Livestock Feeds (Complete feeds and supplements)	2 0 4 2 2 (11 12 13 14 15)	0 1 3 5 (16 17 18 19 20)
B.	Poultry Feeds (Complete feeds and supplements)	2 0 4 2 1 (21 22 23 24 25)	0 1 3 5 (26 27 28 29 30)
C.	Pharmaceutical Preparations for Veterinary Use	2 8 3 4 9 (31 32 33 34 35)	1 3 5 (36 37 38 39 40)
D.		(41 42 43 44 45)	(46 47 48 49 50)
E.		(51 52 53 54 55)	(56 57 58 59 60)
F.		(61 62 63 64 65)	(66 67 68 69 70)
G.		(11 12 13 14 15)	(16 17 18 19 20)
H.		(21 22 23 24 25)	(26 27 28 29 30)
I.		(31 32 33 34 35)	(36 37 38 39 40)
J.		(41 42 43 44 45)	(46 47 48 49 50)
K.		(51 52 53 54 55)	(56 57 58 59 60)
L.		(61 62 63 64 65)	(66 67 68 69 70)
M.		(11 12 13 14 15)	(16 17 18 19 20)
N.		(21 22 23 24 25)	(26 27 28 29 30)
O.		(31 32 33 34 35)	(36 37 38 39 40)

20. Name of Chief Executive Officer George M. Smith Title President

20a. Name of Officer responsible for international activities Albert R. Smith Title Director

21. Cable Address GMSMH-Toronto 22. Telex NA 23. Phone 967-4111

☆ U.S. GOVERNMENT PRINTING OFFICE: 1970—405-003

FIGURE 7.
(Concluded).

PAGE 3 OF 3

WTD on SMITH, George M. and Sons, Toronto, Ontario, Canada
Name and address

24. Firm is controlled by George M. Smith and Sons Albert and Herbert
Name and address of party having controlling interest

25. Financial References National Bank of Canada, Toronto, Ontario, Canada
Names and addresses of banks, etc.

25a. Foreign Participation, if any NA
Countries and percentage of participation

26. Trade References Simpson Laboratories, Canton, Ohio
Names and addresses, preferably of American companies

26a. U.S. Representative K. W. Price Co., 350 Broadway, New York, New York 10007
Name and address

27. Names of major foreign companies represented, or with which licensing arrangements exist, major product lines, and year agencies or licenses were acquired, as reported by subject firm

Name of Company (*Indicate whether agency or licensing arrangement*)	Address (*City, Country*)	Major Product Lines	Year Acquired
Simpson Laboratories (Agency)	Canton, Ohio	Pharmaceutical Preparations for Poultry	1956
Johan Martens Co. (Agency)	Bergen, Norway	Feed Supplements	1958
Denkavit (Agency)	Rotterdam, Netherlands	NA	1966

28. Narrative Description of Firm (**Note**: For importers and distributors, the following factors should be covered whenever possible: location of business, description of building, adequacy of showrooms, technical personnel, servicing and distribution facilities, advertising and sales promotion policies, credit reputation and record, and officers' overall impression of firm. For manufacturers and exporters, the following factors should be covered, as applicable: purchasing and sales policies, plant and production capacities, description of plant equipment and facilities, indication of servicing and distribution facilities, credit reputation and record, nature and description of joint ventures and licensing arrangements). Whenever possible, latest annual report should be submitted as an enclosure, or in lieu thereof the net worth of the firm, if obtainable, should be given.

The firm was originally established as a partnership in 1920 and was reorganized as a corporation in December 1962. George M. Smith (71) and his two sons, Albert (42) and Herbert (45), each own one-third of the capital. The firm maintains a centrally located office and plant with modern facilities. The owners have had considerable technical and administrative experience in this line of business and are well respected in the local business community. The firm wholesales and retails the products it imports, as well as those manufactured in its plant. The sales ability of the company is good throughout Canada. The plant has an annual production capacity of 13,000 metric tons of livestock and poultry feeds and supplements. Actual output in 1969 amounted to 5,500 metric tons. Locally qualified banking and trade sources report that the owners of the firm have a good moral and financial reputation, and that all of the firm's financial obligations are met promptly.

29. Post's Evaluation of Firm (*See item 15*):

The firm has an excellent reputation and is recommended as a trade contact for interested American firms.

30. Preparing Post: Amcongen, Toronto

☆ U.S. GOVERNMENT PRINTING OFFICE: 1970—405-003

Other Approaches

The last few illustrations assumed that a foreign businessman was expressing sufficient interest in American contacts to make his objective known to a Foreign Service commercial officer or to a representative of a private organization able to publicize his interest. What else can we do to find an agent ourselves?

1. We could look over appropriate *Trade Lists* of the Department of Commerce and select names from them to be approached as soon as possible. Trade Lists, compiled by a U.S. Foreign Service post, list firms engaged in specific types of activity in a given country. They are arranged primarily by product, then by the nature of activity surrounding the product: manufacturers, importers, wholesalers, dealers, retailers, and so on, or a combination of these. The lists indicate whether each firm is small, medium-sized, or large, and each name included in the list is supported by specific credit information on the firm in *World Trade Directory Reports*. The Trade Lists do not indicate whether the firms named are currently doing business with U.S. firms or whether the firm is interested in doing so. But one may safely infer that each listed firm is so interested because the detailed information on the firm needed for the *World Trade Directory Reports*, which backstops the Trade Lists, is voluntarily given, and its purpose is known. Figure 8 reproduces part of a Trade List.

2. We could participate in a trade fair in the country selected. A booth could be taken at which our product line could be displayed and seen by businessmen from that and surrounding countries. It would be necessary to have the booth staffed by someone able to discuss representation arrangements and to conduct investigations on the spot as to the candidate's suitability.

3. We could participate in a U.S. Trade Center. These are display centers operated abroad by the Department of Commerce. As of 1971, centers were in operation in London, Frankfurt, Stockholm, Paris, Milan, Tokyo, Bangkok, and Sydney. Each display, which lasts for a month or two, is organized by broad product line, and American businesses are invited to send products for display as possible export items. In the meantime, the commercial attaché will have contacted a wide representation of local businessmen who appear to be potential agents or distributors, informed them of the forthcoming presentation and of the companies and products involved, and invited them to attend. On the other side, background information on the local firms or businesses invited will have been prepared for the use and guidance of the visiting Ameri-

FIGURE 8.
Partial reproduction of a trade list.

A UNITED STATES DEPARTMENT OF COMMERCE PUBLICATION

ID NUMBER: 35400

TRADE LIST
United Kingdom

U.S. DEPARTMENT OF COMMERCE • Bureau of International Commerce • Washington, D.C. 20230

AUGUST 1970 **$1.00**

Machine Tools; Special Dies, Tools, Jigs, Fixtures & Industrial Molds; Machine Tool Accessories; Other Metalworking Machinery

IMPORTERS, DISTRIBUTORS, AGENTS, MANUFACTURERS

This Trade List was compiled by the Department of Commerce from information contained in World Trade Directory Reports prepared by American Foreign Service Officers abroad. Prepared by ADP equipment, the list contains the names of importers, distributors, agents, and, to a lesser extent, manufacturers. The list is designed to assist United States exporters by supplying selective data on trade contacts abroad. It is not intended as a complete list of all the firms in the country in this particular industry.

The firms included herein are listed under each applicable Standard Industrial Classification (SIC) number (1967 manual), together with the corresponding descriptive commodity title. The name of a firm will be repeated under as many commodities as it handles. The complete range of products which each firm handles is indicated by the SIC/Business codes which appear as the last entry of each listing. The types of business codes used in this list are interpreted in column two.

Every effort has been made to include in this list only firms of good repute. However, no responsibility can be assumed by the Government or its officers for any transactions with these firms. Users of this list are urged to utilize the World Trade Directory Report service of the Department to obtain more detailed background information on those firms which may be of particular interest as trade contacts. WTD Reports contain comprehensive information on specific foreign firms with respect to their commercial activities, competence, and reliability. They may be obtained directly from the Bureau of International Commerce, Attn: BIC-924, Washington, D.C. 20230, for $2 per report. A check or money order for the proper amount, made payable to the U.S. Department of Commerce, or the requesting firm's Government Printing Office account number, must accompany each request for WTD Reports.

Persons or firms engaging in international commerce are urged to obtain complete and current market and trade information with respect to foreign countries from the Department of Commerce, or any of its field offices. Consultation with foreign trade specialists in the Department is recommended when specialized assistance in the field of international marketing may be required.

This Trade List contains the following data for each firm to the extent they were available in World Trade Directory Reports: Name and address, name and title of chief executive officer, type of organization, year established, relative size, number of employees, number of salesmen, acceptable language of correspondence, and date of the World Trade Directory Report.

The codes and abbreviations used are as follows:

Business Codes (Type of Business)	Size
0—Manufacturer	Sm—Small
1—Retailer	Md—Medium
2—Agent (sales or indent)	Lg—Large
3—Distributor	VL—Very Large
4—Exporter	
5—Importer	**Language**
6—Cooperative	A—Arabic
7—Engineering	E—English
8—Construction	F—French
9—Other	G—German
	I—Italian
Organization	N—Native
Corp.—Corporation	P—Portuguese
Part.—Partnership	S—Spanish
Prop.—Proprietorship	

Some of the abbreviations used for titles of executive officers are as follows: ADM—administrator; CBD or CHB—chairman of the board; DG—director general; DIR—director; GM—general manager; MD—managing director; OWN—owner; PAR or PTR—partner; PR—president; VP—vice president; TR—treasurer; S—secretary; CPT—Comptroller or controller; M or MGR—manager; SM—sales manager.

If the letters "NA" appear anywhere in this list, they signify that the particular datum is not available.

U KING 35400

SIC NO. 35418 OT MACH TOOLS (PRIM F HOME WORKSHOPS, LAB, ETC.)

NAME, ADDRESS & EXECUTIVE CONTACT	ORGN	ESTAB	SIZE	EMPL	SALES-MAN	LANG	DATE
ARCOY PRODUCTS LIMITED 1/3 KNOWSLEY ROAD BOOTLE 20. LANCASHIRE UK John L. Waite Cbd 35418/04 35482/04	Corp	1963	MD	80	8	N	10/68
CATMUR MACHINE TOOL CORPORATION LTD., 103 LANCASTER ROAD LONDON, W.11 UK Sir William Palmer Cbd 35418/23579 35419/23579 35420/23579	Corp	1950	MD	70	NA	N	02/67
DELAPENA & SON LTD ZONA WORKS, RUSSELL PLACE CHELTENHAM GLOS UK L S Delapena Md 32914/0 35418/04 35673/0 89110/79	Corp	1930	LG	300	12	N	07/67
HERBERT, EDWARD G. LIMITED ATLAS WORKS LEVENSHULME MANCHESTER 19 UK Alan Courtley Md 35410/0245 35418/024 35760/245 38210/245	Corp	1902	MD	500	10	N	09/68
LAMBERTON & COMPANY LIMITED SUNNYSIDE WORKS COATBRIDGE LANARKSHIRE UK J.r. Lamberton Cbd 33620/0 35418/0 35422/0 35423/0 35452/0 35481/0	Corp	1880	MD	300	NA	E	09/68
NOBLE & LUND LIMITED NORTHERN MACHINE TOOL WORKS GATESHEAD COUNTY DURHAM U K H Noble Cbd 35416/0 35418/0 35531/0	Corp	1899	U	NA	NA	N	03/69
ROBERTSON W H A SMALL PARTS LTD ELSTOW WORKS ELSTOW ROAD KEMPSTON BEDFORD BEDS UK M L Boughton Dir 35423/04 35419/04 35418/04	Corp	1932	MD	250	12	N	04/70
RUSSELL, S., & SONS LTD. BATH LANE LEICESTER, LEICS U K S.p. Russell Md 33200/0 35418/04 35420/0	Corp	1864	LG	550	3	N	04/69
TAREX ENGLAND LIMITED 85 RICHFORD STREET LONDON W 6 UK J C Berger Md 35415/352 35418/352	Corp	1956	MD	22	5	N	06/69
WICKMAN WIMET LTD P O BOX 63, TORRINGTON AVENUE TILE HILL COVENTRY WARWICKS. U K H B Morris Cbd 35324/014 35413/014 35418/014 35419/014 35441/014	Corp	1940	LG	1200	NA	N	06/67

SIC NO. 35419 PTS F MET CUTT MACH TOOLS, SOLD SEP, & REBUILT MACH

NAME, ADDRESS & EXECUTIVE CONTACT	ORGN	ESTAB	SIZE	EMPL	SALES-MAN	LANG	DATE
BURROWS & SMITH LIMITED SAFFRON LANE LEICESTER LE2 6UH UK J D Burrows Cbd 35410/0 35416/0 35419/0 35199/0	Corp	1940	MD	250	3	N	01/70
CATMUR MACHINE TOOL CORPORATION LTD., 103 LANCASTER ROAD LONDON, W.11 UK Sir William Palmer Cbd 35418/23579 35419/23579 35420/23579	Corp	1950	MD	70	NA	N	02/67
CLIFFORD MACHINE TOOLS LIMITED CHERRYWOOD ROAD BIRMING HAM UK R. T. Williams Gm 35419/0 35441/0 35442/0	Corp	1945	SM	NA	NA	N	02/67
COXS MACHINERY LTD. VICTORIA TERRACE ST PHILIPS MARSH BRISTOL P S Henman Dir 35419/04 35424/04 35513/045 35552/045 35593/045 35595/045 35615/045 36000/78	Corp	1938	MD	75	NA	E	05/66
FRENCHAY PRODUCTS LTD. STATION ROAD BRISTOL UK E.r.m. Faye Cbd 35419/07 35424/07 89110/9	Corp	1949	MD	150	NA	N	10/68
ROBERTSON W H A SMALL PARTS LTD ELSTOW WORKS ELSTOW ROAD KEMPSTON BEDFORD BEDS UK M L Boughton Dir 35423/04 35419/04 35418/04	Corp	1932	MD	250	12	N	04/70
WARD THOMAS W. LIMITED ALBION WORKS, SAVILLE STREET, SHEFFIELD 4 YORKSHIRE UK H. W. Secker Cbd 33521/0 34521/0 35319/0 35370/0 35419/0 35592/0 35595/0 35891/0	Corp	1904	VL	12000	NA	N	03/67
WICKMAN WIMET LTD P O BOX 63, TORRINGTON AVENUE TILE HILL COVENTRY WARWICKS. U K H B Morris Cbd 35324/014 35413/014 35418/014 35419/014 35441/014	Corp	1940	LG	1200	NA	N	06/67
WICKSTEED, CHARLES & CO. LTD. STAMFORD ROAD WORKS KETTERING J Didsdall Dir 33210/04 33220/04 35419/04 35450/04 35590/04 39492/04 39493/04	Corp	1876	LG	NA	NA	E	04/66

SIC NO. 35420 METAL-FORMING MACHINE TOOLS

NAME, ADDRESS & EXECUTIVE CONTACT	ORGN	ESTAB	SIZE	EMPL	SALES-MAN	LANG	DATE
ADAM & HARVEY LIMITED STANDARD HOUSE LONDON E C 2 UK P Adam Cbd 22310/04 24210/345 33200/345 33600/345 35420/345 37112/345 37113/345	Corp	1946	LG	300	6	N	03/69
ADDISON TOOL CO LTD EASTWOOD STREET MITCHAM LANE LONDON S W 16 UK E N Addison Dir 35320/52 35410/52 35420/52	Corp	1956	MD	30	NA	N	06/69
AUTOMATION LIMITED BESSEMER ROAD BASINGSTOKE, HAMPSHIRE UK G. E. H. Marbaix Md 35414/02 35420/02 35480/02 35485/02	Corp	1954	MD	NA	NA	N	06/68
BALL PLASTICS LTD BURSTEAD WORKS KENNEL LANE BILLERICAY U K J E Ball Cbd 30790/03 35450/03 35420/03 36000/03 36120/03 34710/09	Corp	1921	MD	775	11	N	03/70
BROOMFIELD ENGINEERING COMPANY LIMITED FOLLY HALL HUDDERSFIELD YORKSHIRE Ralph C Charlesworth Na 35410/0 35420/0 35441/0 35450/0 35452/0	Corp	1950	MD	95	3	E	12/66
CATMUR MACHINE TOOL CORPORATION LTD., 103 LANCASTER ROAD LONDON, W.11 UK Sir William Palmer Cbd 35418/23579 35419/23579 35420/23579	Corp	1950	MD	70	NA	N	02/67
CENGAR UNIVERSAL TOOL CO. LTD. PO BOX 34 7 HORTON STREET HALIFAX Jack W Sutcliffe Na 35410/07 35420/07	Corp	1945	U	NA	NA	E	02/66
CLIFTON & BAIRD LIMITED EMPRESS WORKS JOHNSTONE RENFREWSHIRE UK G Morrison Hay Cbd 35416/0 35420/0 35450/0	Corp	1908	MD	80	NA	N	03/69
CROWBOROUCH ENGINEERING FACTORY 10A17 AVENUE AYCLIFFE INDUSTRIALS ESTATE DARLINGTON CO DURHAM E Garnjost Dir 35000/04 35300/04 35320/04 35352/04 35410/04 35420/04 35441/04 35450/04	Corp	1943	LG	NA	NA	E	02/66
DARWINS MAGNETIC PRODUCTS LTD. FITZWILLIAM WORKS TINSLEY SHEFFIELD 9 Mark R Balfour Dir 35420/0 36520/0 36620/0 36790/0 38110/0 38210/0	Corp	1944	MD	NA	NA	E	10/66
DAVIS STUART, MACHINES LIMITED NORFOLK STREET COVENTRY WARWICKSHIRE UK Douglas D. Davis Md 35420/02 35662/02	Corp	1966	MD	NA	NA	N	11/67
E.G.B. TOOL AND EQUIPMENT COMPANY LIMITED 1 GOLDERS GREEN ROAD LONDON, N.W. 11. UK E.g. Budwig Md 35420/35 35480/35	Corp	1965	SM	4	2	N	11/68
ELECTRO-CHEMICAL ENGINEERING CO. LTD. FORSYTHE ROAD SHEERWATER WOKING	Corp	1939	LG	400	NA	E	10/66

can businessmen. In this way a number of potential and mutually interested contacts will have been established. The record of this promotional program is that a substantial number of orders have been reported by American firms exhibiting in trade centers. The centers thus serve not only as places where agencies and distributorships may be cultivated, but where new products can be displayed in support of already existing representation. The first trade center opened in London in June 1961, and up to March 1970 there had been 300 different trade center shows at the several trade centers. The results of this activity were: [5]

Total sales during the exhibitions and between-show promotions: $58.2 million
Total sales by firms resulting from trade center operations in the first year after exhibiting: $379.5 million
Total U.S. firms exhibiting: 9,886
Total registered visitors: 402,259
Total exhibitions: 300

4. We could participate in trade missions. In recent years, two kinds of trade missions have been undertaken with official backing. One is government-organized; the other is industry-organized. The missions consist mostly of businessmen but the full support of the U.S. commercial officers abroad facilitates the makeup of itinerary, introductions, publicity, and so on.

5. We could have a trade contact survey made by requesting it of the Department of Commerce, which then gives the responsibility to the commercial attaché of the country concerned. It involves bringing an American firm's export interest to the attention of a selected number of foreign firms, which are then interviewed to determine whether they are interested in representing the American firm. The Foreign Service does not select the successful foreign firm, but attempts to submit three final names to the American firm, with supporting data. The American firm can then make its own selection, after making any additional investigation it wishes.

When a potential list has been narrowed down to a few names, the job is to select only one, and the potential exporter should therefore get to know the candidates in some way other than by letter. The ideal way is a trip to the foreign market, after investigation of both the market and the individual firms being considered. Unfortunately this is not always possible.

---

[5] U.S. Department of Commerce, *International Commerce*, March 30, 1970, p. 18.

But if credit and competence checking are satisfactory and the field is narrowed down through correspondence and personal interview, one representative is chosen with whom to work out an agency or other representation agreement. As indicated earlier, he is, or should be, as interested in the details of the contract as we are, and the ideal thing to do, in the eyes of many experienced exporters, is to investigate and discuss before the agreement is made, draw up the contract, put it into the safe, and hope it will never have to be referred to.

Continuing Liaison with Foreign Representatives

Once a foreign representative has been named, effective liaison must be established with him in what is to be a cooperative undertaking. He and no one else, except for reserved segments (parts of a market not given to an agent to handle), is the channel of distribution in the market assigned to him by contract. Two steps to achieve this are basic: a sales action plan or program, and effective communications between the representative and the home office.

Since the original contract itself cannot spell out sales targets or quotas for several years ahead, this aspect of market development must be attended to periodically and in relation to the immediate outlook. A sales program must be realistic and agreed upon, if not worked out jointly, because from the exporter's point of view, resources for production and anticipated income from sales must be budgeted; and from the foreign representative's point of view, he must put together the necessary distribution organization and be assured of adequate and anticipated supply for a planned volume within an agreed-upon price structure (which itself may change from time to time) and with allowance for satisfactory operating margin.

A foreign representative certainly does not want to be held accountable for not having reached an unrealistic goal or target imposed on him. New products, or products new to a given market, require time to be introduced and accepted. They may not pay off for two or three years. What is needed is a practical forecast or estimated goal, companion to which is agreement on direct or supportive participation by the exporter in the marketing effort. Included here are considerations such as advertising, training of foreign personnel by the exporter (when, for how long, at whose expense, and so on), display and promotion (participation in trade fairs or other promotional devices, preparation and provision of appropriately translated foreign sales manuals and other literature), and after-sales servicing or attention as necessary. All these factors contribute to aggressive attention by the representative abroad, what may be termed dealer loyalty, which, if achieved, reduces the need for close control.

Any estimate of market potential, if translated into an immediate target that can be used as a measure of performance, must be worked out with the foreign representative, for he is the man whose performance is being measured. He must agree to the target or say why he cannot meet it. This involves a continuous flow of information through the distribution system. Information flows down on matters such as proper display of the product, presentation, sales and servicing, questions raised occasionally as to the amount of attention given to it, the amount of space and sales effort given over by the representative and his organization to this product, and any expansion in facilities or area coverage if called for. Information flowing up could deal with business conditions, government policies affecting the market for the product, local production, the activities of competing exporters, new products on the market, advisable modifications, reactions or observations of customers and potential customers, in fact, all feedback from the market to the exporter.

When it comes to evaluating a representative's effort and performance, consider points such as the representative's sending in adequate reports and current market and economic information, always changing because of such uncontrollables as import quotas, currency regulations, trade barriers, foreign competition, tax considerations, and the like.

The representative's actual sales results may be evaluated through indicators such as his share of market, if available; by his current as against his past performance, with due allowance for changing conditions; and by performance against market survey targets. The continuous market research underlying the end objective can thus be a joint or shared effort between the home office and foreign representatives, leading to suggested product modification or price/margin adjustments as well as to better-directed and more effective marketing efforts in the respective foreign markets.

9

Importing

Most of what has been covered so far pertains to exports, and because in many ways importing is the reverse operation, to some degree the problems and procedures in both are the same. However, there are many significant differences, both operational and institutional. In both, obstacles and formalities are numerous. But in importing, the principal laws and institutions as well as the market to be satisfied are American rather than foreign.

SIGNIFICANCE OF IMPORTS TO THE ECONOMY

Imports are vital to the economy as a whole because they serve to maintain and raise a nation's standards of living. Indeed, some people argue that the greatest gain in international trade comes from imports rather than exports because, through importing, goods can be obtained that are not producible domestically or can be acquired at lower cost than if produced domestically. Moreover, specific imports are vital to specific nations, and are even more vital to specific industries and companies. Imports provide the base for employment, either in the processing of the imported product or in its transportation and trading activity. In order to appreciate the position of imports in the United States economy and the impact of imports on U.S. international economic relations, a number of quantitative measures can be utilized. Primary among these is simply the identification of some of the most important U.S. imports in terms of dollar volume. For 1970, they were as shown in Table 11.

However, the importance of imports to an economy may rest on considerations other than that of purely dollar amounts. Chief among these is the reliance a country's economy places on specific imports in relation to its own production of that product or product-type. In this connection, Figure 9 indicates the value of imports and new supply (domestic production plus imports) for selected 4-digit commodity groups each of whose imports are 10 percent or more of new supply and are valued at more than $50 million.[1] The Department of Commerce calculated that for 1967, imports provided 10 percent or more of new supply in some 35 4-digit Standard Industrial Classification commodity groups. Some are strategically important and are available in major part only from foreign sources.

A number of products that contribute to an improvement in the American standard of living are available substantially only through imports. These include coffee, cocoa, bananas, certain oilseeds and fibers, chromium, industrial diamonds, and a few specialties such as champagne, French and German wines, Scotch whisky, and perfumes. Imports, moreover, have a direct impact on the overall international relations of the United States, as indicated by the importance of the United States as a market for the exports of several countries. This is shown in Table 12. More than ten countries depend on the United States to absorb a third or more of

---

[1] U.S. Department of Commerce, *U.S. Commodity Exports and Imports as Related to Output*, 1967 and 1966, 1970, p. 4.

Table 11. Principal U.S. imports, 1963–1970 ($ million).

Imports	*1963–1970 ($ million)*		*Percent of 1970 Total*	
Food and live animals		5,379		13.4
Fish	794		2.0	
Sugar	729		1.8	
Coffee	1,160		2.9	
Cocoa	201		0.5	
Beverages and tobacco		855		2.1
Crude materials, inedible, except fuels		3,312		8.3
Rubber	236		0.6	
Wood pulp	480		1.2	
Iron ore and concentrates	480		1.2	
Mineral fuels and related materials		3,081		7.7
Petroleum and products	2,770		6.9	
Animal and vegetable oils and fats		160		0.4
Chemicals		1,450		3.6
Machinery and transport equipment		11,171		30.0
Nonelectric machinery	3,017		7.5	
Office machines	505		1.3	
Electrical apparatus	2,272		5.7	
Passenger cars	3,719		9.3	
Manufactured goods classified by material		8,437		21.1
Paper, paperboard, and manufactures	1,087		2.7	
Iron and steel	2,032		5.1	
Nonferrous base metals	2,501		3.8	
Textiles, excluding fibers and apparel	1,135		2.8	
Clothing, excluding footwear		1,267		3.2

SOURCE: U.S. Department of Commerce, *Foreign Trade* (FT 990), December 1970, Table I-2, 1971.

their sales abroad and those sending 10 percent or more of their exports to the United States number close to 20.

The connection between imports and employment is more tenuous than that between exports and employment, which is often obvious. A few years ago, the Department of Labor concluded that about 940,000 U.S. workers were supported in 1960 by activities connected with imports into the United States.

IMPORT ORGANIZATION

In importing, one is obtaining or receiving goods. An importer does not produce or manufacture them, unless they come from a

FIGURE 9.
Values of imports and new supply for selected 4-digit commodity groups.

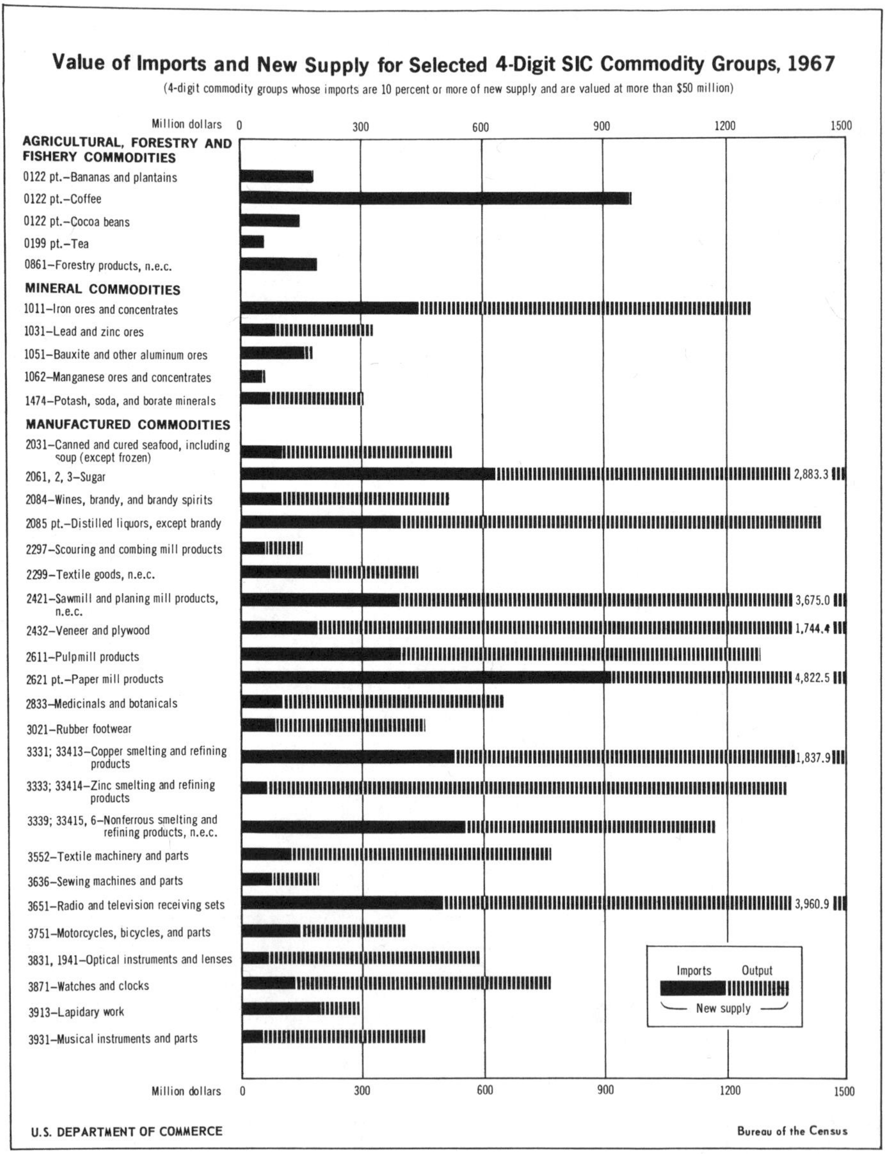

Table 12. Principal country sources of U.S. imports in 1969.

	Imports ($ million)	*Exports to U.S. as Percent of Total Exports*
Canada	10,390	68
Japan	4,388	32
Germany	2,603	10
United Kingdom	2,121	14
Italy	1,204	11
Mexico	1,029	65
Venezuela	940	33
France	842	6
Hong Kong	815	34
Belgium-Luxembourg	684	9
Brazil	616	33
Australia	588	14
Netherlands	467	5
Switzerland	452	10
Philippines	423	45
China (Taiwan)	388	36
Sweden	355	8
India	344	17
Peru	313	40
Malaysia	307	n.a.*
Spain	304	18
Korea	291	52
Denmark	258	8
South Africa	243	7
Colombia	240	42

SOURCE: U.S. Department of Commerce, *Overseas Business Reports* 70-3, Tables 6 and 13, 1970.

* Not available.

branch or subsidiary of the parent importer. He merely buys them, so the size of organization needed to accomplish this task is minimal. Importers (as buyers) in most product lines are sought out by sellers, or there are easy and convenient markets in which to buy. Being on the receiving end enables one to observe, perhaps more clearly than in exporting, the difference between operational procedures for goods that are typically *sold,* that is, those that are not unique, and goods that must be *marketed,* that is, those that are unique or specialized.

Buying is relatively easy, even the buying related to imports. The big problem in much of importing is *selling*. Depending on the type of product, some selling is done well in advance of importing (on a sample or classification basis, for example) and some goods are sold while en route, either having been purchased by the importer or being transported on consignment or as inventory by a domestic unit of a foreign producer or seller.

Organizationally, there is a high degree of functional similarity between export and import distribution channels. Both include professional foreign traders: import merchants, import brokers, and import commission houses. Import merchants, trading for their own account and risk, can be found in almost any field, handling any of the whole range of merchandise, from raw materials to finished products.

Brokers are an important import channel in terms of dollar import volume, because they engage in big-volume, bulk commodities such as sugar, wool, metals, oils, coffee, cocoa, and rubber. An import broker commonly brings in goods in his own name, sometimes on consignment, and arranges for direct payment to the seller. The import broker acts for the foreign seller. Brokers play a prominent role in moving goods under consignment to highly organized or concentrated markets.

Import commission houses, which function in the interest of the foreign exporter, offer display rooms for sample goods, especially the type handled by department stores and the type traded on the basis of samples. In import markets as large and important as the United States or certain European centers, and wherever volume justifies, one also finds branches or agents of foreign producers. This goes for raw materials as well as finished goods, from, say, Chilean nitrates and cocoa to Volkswagens.

On the more aggressive and selective side, a very important institutional segment in import trade is that consisting of purchasing agents or resident buyers permanently stationed abroad. This is a particularly active element in the movement of finished consumer goods, such as those handled by department stores. In Paris and other large centers, buying offices function for such well-known American stores as Macy's, Marshall Field & Company, Saks, Gimbel's, and Sears Roebuck and Company. Some of these buy for a number of large American outlets usually related in a corporate way in the United States. For example, Gimbel-Saks Purchasing, S.A., in Paris, serves as buying agent for several stores in its group within the United States, among which are Saks & Co. (New York and other cities), Gimbel Brothers (New York and other cities), and Neiman Marcus (Dallas). Also active in this area are resident buyers for groups of stores. Adolphe Schloss Fils et Cie., of Paris, is the channel for reaching such well-known American outlets as I. Magnin and Company, Abercrombie & Fitch, Julius Garfinckel Company, Sakowitz Inc. in Houston, and A. Harris in Dallas. Some resident buyers purchase centrally within the United States; among this type of buying organization are the stores affiliated with Associated Merchandising Corporation.

Quite significant is the direct import activity by manufacturers and traders, either from their own production abroad or from representatives or buying agents stationed abroad. Typical of products moving in large volumes through this channel are primary materials, such as bauxite, copper, coffee, iron ore, newsprint, petroleum, and waxes; and manufactured goods such as glassware, radios, and automobiles. Some of these move from foreign subsidiaries to American parents but goods moving in from other countries, even though intercompany transactions, are legally imports. For example, General Motors' bringing in Opel automobiles for sale in the United States means imports, even though the products were made by its own subsidiary abroad, just as General Motors' shipping of Chevrolets to its own subsidiaries in other countries constitutes exports.

Even though the activity of those interested in importing —importers, domestic manufacturers, servicing functions such as banks, customhouse brokers, attorneys, and transportation companies—varies widely and will not always engage their full-time interest, sufficient communality of interest exists to underlie the formation and work of the American Importers Association, headquartered in New York. This association develops positions on import problems and policies, testifies on legislation affecting imports, and otherwise presents the concerted view of those most directly engaged in the importing process. The New York *Journal of Commerce* publishes a directory of United States and Canadian importers, identifying their key executives, bank references, merchandise handled, and annual volumes. The 1971 edition lists about 30,000 firms.

To complete the circle of coverage one must recognize simply that an importer needs dependable sources and must be in direct touch with them. He therefore needs as much or as little of an organization as will make this direct linkage with the foreign market secure and smooth. Unless he is buying for an assured market, he also will need a selling organization to dispose of what he has imported. A distinction can be drawn between indirect and direct exporting, but the linkage between American importers and foreign suppliers must be direct. Direct contact, as used here, includes contact with offices or representatives of foreign suppliers stationed in the United States whose job it is to represent a foreign exporter and put him in touch with American buyers.

PHYSICAL ROUTING OF IMPORTS

The center of import trade in the United States, at least as far as variety is concerned, is New York, although most large port cities and a number of interior trading centers include some importers. The importance of ports and port areas as the location of import activity was brought out a few years ago by a study of the Department of Commerce. This survey, dealing with waterborne exports and imports, found that in the year studied (1956), 60 percent of import tonnage was consigned to destinations inside the port area (defined as within ten miles from the center of city in which the port was located) and 13 percent to destinations within 100 miles of the port. Excluded from the survey were certain large-tonnage products, such as sugar, bananas, pulpwood, crude petroleum, residual fuel oil, iron ore and concentrates, manganese, chrome, and aluminum ores and concentrates.

However, this does not necessarily represent the geographical

Table 13. U.S. general imports entering through principal customs districts in 1969.

Customs District	*$ Millions*
New York	9,251
Detroit	3,676
Buffalo	2,681
Los Angeles	2,482
Philadelphia	1,730
San Francisco	1,241
New Orleans	1,224
Chicago	1,130
Seattle	1,129
Baltimore	1,107
Ogdensburg, N.Y.	1,025
Boston	846

SOURCE: U.S. Department of Commerce, *Highlights of U.S. Export and Import Trade* (FT 990), December 1969, Table 1-5, 1970, p. 88.

Table 14. U.S. general imports entering through principal customs districts in 1969 (thousands of tons)

Customs District	*By Vessel*	*By Air*
Philadelphia	109,191	6.8
New York	107,382	302.8
Baltimore	40,570	5.7
New Orleans	33,776	4.5
San Juan, P.R.	25,586	22.0
Boston	23,250	29.4
Los Angeles	22,714	31.6
Cleveland	20,856	1.5
Mobile	18,858	—
Tampa	16,643	0.6
Norfolk	16,218	—
Galveston	14,949	—
San Francisco	14,900	37.7
Chicago	13,865	32.0
Seattle	11,469	5.9

SOURCE: U.S. Department of Commerce, *Highlights of U.S. Export and Import Trade* (FT 990), December 1969, Table 1-5, 1970, p. 88.

routes through which imports physically enter the United States and at which points much of the procedural handling and documentation take place. In 1969 general imports entering the United States came in through the customs districts shown in Table 13. By shipping weight, the principal customs districts through which merchandise entered were as shown in Table 14. Tables 13 and 14 reflect differences in the routing of small physical volume, but high-dollar-value items and bulk items, many of which, per pound, are nowhere as costly as finished goods. However, both give rise to the same procedural problems concerned with entry into the United States.

ADMINISTRATIVE CONTROLS OVER IMPORTING

Import operations must be conducted within a framework of commercial policy that permits, encourages, regulates, or prohibits trade opportunities. The various policies, based on laws and regulations, are made effective through administrative procedures whose purpose it is to assure that goods whose entry is prohibited do not enter; goods that do enter conform to applicable rules and regulations; customs duties and other applicable taxes are collected in the proper amount and at the proper time; necessary statistical intelligence concerning imports is promptly and correctly gathered; and the rights of the importer as a taxpayer and of the collector of customs as a tax gatherer are protected, through adversary proceedings, if necessary.

TARIFFS

Government impediments to imports are commonly grouped into two categories: tariffs and nontariff trade barriers. Customs duties, or tariffs, are a form of tax imposed by all countries against imported goods. This is one of the oldest forms of taxation, one reason for which is ease of collection, effected when goods physically cross a national frontier.

The base on which a duty is levied is one of three measurements: physical units of the goods, monetary value of the goods, or a combination of the two. These customs duties are usually referred to as *specific, ad valorem,* and *compound,* respectively. Prior to imposing the tax, however, there must be agreement between the taxpayer and the tax gatherer as to what the imported item is, for duty and statistical purposes. This is known as *classification.* Rate of duty depends on identity and classification of a product. For example, if one imports a mechanical pencil with a cigarette lighter at one end, what is it, a pencil or a lighter? Classification becomes important when the rate of duty applicable to two possible classifications is significantly different; it is a matter of some consequence if the tariff rate is 50 percent rather than 20 percent.

Once an item is classified, the type of duty can be determined. At this point some problems may arise. For instance, if the duty applicable is *ad valorem,* its value must be determined *for duty purposes.* This should be simple, using the commercial invoice, but it is not. The law clearly specifies the value basis to be used, which may very well differ from the transaction price on the invoice. (Under Section 402 of the Tariff Act of 1930, as amended, the basis of valuation for customs purposes is as follows, except as otherwise specifically provided for: the export value; if the export value cannot be determined satisfactorily, then the U.S. value; if neither the export value nor the U.S. value can be determined satisfactorily, then the constructed value, except that in the case of an imported article subject to a rate of duty based on the American selling price, such value shall be the American selling price of such domestic article. The section contains detailed definitions of each of these values.)

The invoice may be in terms of U.S. dollars or of the currency of the country of exportation, or even of a third currency. When prices are stated in foreign currencies, they must be converted to U.S. dollars in order to arrive at appropriate import valuations, whether the goods are dutiable or not. (The rate to be used is basically the noon buying rate on the day of exportation for cable transfers payable in the foreign currency to be converted. The rate is determined by the Federal Reserve Bank of New York and certified to the secretary of the treasury. See Section 522 of the Tariff Act of 1930.)

Specific duties based on physical measurement of goods—weight, liquid measure, or distance—are easiest to collect. But their use is objected to in some quarters because the impact, or burden, changes with price. For example, a 10¢ per unit duty applied against an item worth $1 equals a 10 percent duty. But if the market value of the product should fall to 50¢, the burden would be 20 percent, whereas if the market rose to $2, it would be only 5 percent. So, the amount of protection provided is least when prices are high, a time when foreign exporters might be attracted to the U.S. market, and greatest when prices in the United States are low, when the market might not be so attractive to foreign exporters and the pressure to purchase abroad by U.S. importers should be less noticeable.

Specific duties cannot be used for many products because economic significance is not related to physical measurement. For example, there is no reason to expect that ten pounds of scientific instruments are equal in any way other than by weight to ten pounds of any other scientific instruments, and one may be many times more valuable than the other.

Ad valorem duties are the only satisfactory ones for certain products because they accomplish the double objective of providing protection and revenue, yet they provide some basis for spreading of burden. However, a tax that is uniform in proportion to value may be criticized as bearing more heavily on those who are by necessity the consumers of low-value products. Thus it may be looked on as regressive.

Because some processed products are dutiable in proportion to value while the material from which they are made is dutiable in terms of physical measurement, the use of a compound duty has evolved. This duty is assessable at say, so much per pound, plus a certain percentage of value. Thus a manufacturer who would have to pay a duty on imported raw materials is given added protection by having his foreign competition made to pay the same duty as he does on raw materials used in the making of a finished product for the United States market.

One example of compound duty used by the United States in mid-1971 is hand-woven fabrics of wool, with a loom width of less than 30 inches and weighing not over 4 ounces per square yard. The duty is 30¢ per pound plus 15 percent *ad valorem*. Another example is scissors and shears, valued at over $1.75 per dozen. The duty is 10¢ each plus 22.5 percent *ad valorem*.

Tariff Schedules of the United States

All imports into the United States are subject to duty unless specifically exempted. In the United States tariff arrangement there was for many years a dutiable list and a free list and, although the president was authorized under the reciprocal trade agreements program to modify actual rates of duty within specified limits, he was not at first given authority to remove any item from the dutiable list and place it on the free list, nor to impose a duty on goods that Congress had decided would be importable into the United States duty-free.

Under the Trade Expansion Act of 1962, the president was authorized to reduce the duty to zero if the level of duty were only of nuisance value—say 5 percent or less *ad valorem*—and he was also authorized to eliminate duty on certain tropical products if the European Common Market also eliminated their duties on the same products.

The Tariff Schedules of the United States are the official and legal schedule of United States duties, and include notations, where appropriate, that the listed item is duty-free. In order to consolidate information on taxes on or impediments to imports other than the duty rate, and to serve as a guide to the statistical reporting requirements imposed on importers, the official Tariff Schedules have been extended into the *Tariff Schedules of the United States (Annotated)*. In many cases statistical identification is more detailed than necessary for determining applicable duty.

Levels of Duty

Ever since the concept began of exchanging reductions in tariff rates through negotiation, there has been a question of whether the United States (or any other country for that matter) gains as much as it gives up in any negotiation. The technical difficulty of reaching a quantitative estimate is complicated by the need to reduce all tariffs to an *ad valorem* equivalency. A specific rate, reduced to a percentage of value, will appear higher or lower, depending on whether the prices of goods subject to a specific duty are lower or higher at the times being compared. The same complication pertains to the specific portion of compound duties.

However, reductions of all types of duty to a common denominator are attractive from two views: indicating whether there is an equivalence of trade-off in tariff reductions and concessions received, and estimating the historical evolution of any nation's level of tariffs, a quantitative estimation of which is also affected by the composition, in terms of dutiable and duty-free imports, of its import trade. This is further complicated by the existence of more than one rate of duty, depending on the country of origin. Here the simple question, to which there is no simple answer, is whether a nation is a high- or a low-tariff country; and what direction it is moving in, quantitatively.

The closest estimate of the level of United States import duties appears to be that developed annually by the Department of Commerce, wherein the total of duties collected is divided by total imports and by dutiable imports in order to develop a percentage level of duties in terms of all imports or only of dutiable imports.

The record over the past four decades is shown in Table 15.

Table 15. Ratios of duties collected to value of imports entered for consumption, 1926–1969.

Yearly Average or Year	*Duties Collected as*	
	Percent of Total Imports	*Percent of Dutiable Imports*
1926–1930	14	40
1931–1935	18	50
1936–1940	15	38
1941–1945	11	32
1946–1950	4	16
1951–1955	5	12
1956–1960	7	11
1961–1965	7	12
1966	8	12
1967	8	12
1968	7	11
1969	7	11

SOURCE: U.S. Department of Commerce, *Statistical Abstract of the United States*, Table 1220, 1970.

These statistics should be accepted guardedly. One should take into account the effect not only of changes in prices but also of changes in the pattern of import trade, that is, whether the duty-free volume is increasing or decreasing relative to the total volume of imports.

Although our main interest here is imports, it would be appropriate to recognize that the deliberate reduction of United States tariffs was undertaken as a step toward opening foreign markets for United States exports. That is why the original trade agreements bill (Section 350 of the Tariff Act of 1930) is titled "Promotion of Foreign Trade." On this point it is appropriate to ask whether reductions in United States duty rates, undertaken as a trade-off to open foreign markets for United States exports, did in fact contribute to a greater or lesser increase in imports relative to exports. Clearly the intervening war and its aftermath of economic and political upheavals were strong and probably dominant contributing factors to the pattern of United States foreign trade, but Table 16 lends a basis for suggesting that, overall, the reciprocal trade agreements program was a success, and that the United States is better off because of it.

Table 16. Export and import growth since beginning of reciprocal trade agreements program ($ million).

	1931–1935 Average	*1965–1969 Average*	*Increase (Times)*
Imports for consumption	1,704	28,462	16.70
Exports (total domestic)	1,989	31,961	16.07
Exports (excluding military grant-aid)		31,249	15.71
Average increase in imports		26,780	
Average increase in exports (excluding military grant-aid)		29,260	

Table 16 shows that in terms of dollars, exports did increase more than imports, although imports increased more in terms of percent, because the relation is to a smaller base. This reflects the very large increase in imports into the United States in 1969, part of which was caused by the level of both economic activity and inflated prices in the United States. In the five years 1963–1967 and 1964–1968, the proportionate increase and the monetary increase in exports were larger than for imports.

The foregoing liberal use of statistics is not intended as proof of any causal influence, especially that of the overall reduction of tariffs on a mutual negotiated basis. But it does give the impression that the whole program has accomplished its goals, making allowance for the many other causative factors bearing on the volume and direction of international trade.

Special and Additional Import Duties

The two best examples of special and additional duties applicable to imports, and then on a contingency basis, are the *countervailing* and the *antidumping* duties. Countervailing duties are imposable only against imports that are subject to duty under the Tariff Act or subject to an import tax under provisions of the Internal Revenue Code. They are intended to offset a subsidy paid to foreign firms exporting to the United States. As of early 1970, the countervailing duties in effect were as shown in Table 17.

Table 17. Countervailing duties in effect in United States as of early 1970.

Country	*Commodity*
Australia	Sugar content of certain articles, butter
Canada	Certain types of cheese
Cuba	Cordage
Denmark	Butter
France	Canned tomato paste
Great Britain	Certain spirits, sugar
Ireland	Spirits
Italy	Canned tomatoes and canned tomato concentrates, galvanized fabricated structural steel units for erection of electrical transmission towers, steel welded wire mesh, ski-lifts and parts thereof, certain steel products

SOURCE: National Archives and Records Service, *Code of Federal Regulations*, Title 19, revised as of January 1, 1970, pp. 332–333.

Antidumping duties can be imposed on imported merchandise, whether dutiable or free, if:

1. The product is being sold in the United States at less than fair value; that is, when the purchase price or exporter's sales price is less than the price at which such merchandise is sold for consumption in the country of exportation; or, if consumption is so small in that country as not to provide an adequate basis for comparison, the price at which such merchandise is sold for exportation to countries other than the United States. (See *Customs Regulations of the United States*, 14 N 15).

2. If importation threatens a domestic industry or prevents one from being established.

The duty collectible is equal either to the difference between the purchase price (or exporter's sales price) and the price at which sold in the country of production; or, if the product is not sold in the home market, or sold in such small numbers as to be an inadequate basis for comparison, the difference between prices to the United States and prices for exportation to third countries. Much of the basic information on price, which is the initial evidence needed in an investigation, is called for by the special customs invoice (see Chapter 6). One objection to this form is that a foreign exporter frequently cannot answer the questions asked. Antidumping duties were in force in mid-1970 against the imports from sources listed in Table 18.

Table 18. Findings of dumping in the United States in effect as of early 1970.

Country	*Merchandise*
Australia	Chromic acid
Belgium	Portland cement, other than white
Canada	Potassium chloride, steel reinforcing bars, carbon steel bars and structural shapes, steel jacks
Czechoslovakia	Pig iron
Dominican Republic	Portland cement, other than white
East Germany	Pig iron
France	Potassium chloride
Portugal	Portland gray cement
Rumania	Pig iron
Sweden	Portland cement, other than white
USSR	Pig iron, titanium sponge
West Germany	Potassium chloride

SOURCE: National Archives and Records Service, *Code of Federal Regulations*, Title 19, revised as of January 1, 1970, p. 523.

Two additional import duties that are provided for but that have not been imposed to date are a duty to equalize costs of production between a foreign country and the United States (Section 336 of the Tariff Act of 1930); and an antidiscrimination duty (Section 338 of the Tariff Act of 1930). The former lost much of its usefulness when actual rates of duty began to be negotiated and set by the president within limits specified by Congress, because the law refers to duties expressly fixed by statute as those intended to be increased in order to equalize production costs. The original Act has now been amended to exclude its applicability to any article whose importation into the United States has been negotiated by a foreign trade agreement.

Insofar as Section 338 is concerned, the additional duty that can be imposed to counter discrimination is not to exceed 50 percent *ad valorem,* or its equivalent, on products of, or articles imported in a vessel of, the foreign country found to have discriminated directly or indirectly against the commerce of the United States. Besides imposing this additional duty, the president is authorized to exclude such products from importation. As of late 1971, this measure of protection had not been employed, the complaints having been handled and relief having been obtained through negotiation and suasion.

Still another duty is authorized by Section 22 of the Agricultural Adjustment Act. Under this law an additional 50 percent *ad valorem* duty can be imposed when necessary to prevent imports of the articles under consideration from materially interfering with domestic agricultural programs. Besides this possible 50 percent additional duty, the president is authorized to impose quantitative limitations within certain bounds in order to achieve the same objective.

Other examples of special and additional duties imposed by the United States as of mid-1971 were those applicable against iron or steel products which contain, by weight, specified portions of chromium, molybdenum, tungsten, or vanadium; each jewel on clocks valued at over $10; sugars, syrups, and molasses, for such time as the tax imposed under Sec. 4501, Internal Revenue Code, is in effect (the tax terminates June 30, 1972).

Imported goods are subject to the same special taxes as domestically produced goods. Typical are federal excise taxes and state and local sales taxes. Other taxes applied against imported goods over and above customs duty are internal revenue taxes, regulatory taxes, processing taxes, and import taxes. The latter two were repealed by Section 302 (d) of the Tariff Classification Act of 1962.

NONTARIFF TRADE BARRIERS

Perhaps the topic that has engendered most interest in commercial policy in the last decade is the nontariff barrier to imports, because levels of duty have been negotiated downward and are no longer an impossible barrier to trade. One can make up his own definition as to what a nontariff barrier is. A simple one is "a financial impediment that is not a customs duty," or "a nonfinancial impediment, such as quantitative limitations on imports and prior import deposits." (Prior import deposits are required in some countries; that is, their importers must deposit with a designated government authority or bank the cost of imports in advance of importation. In some countries the deposit must be well in advance and in some it must be more than the estimated cost of imports. The objective in requiring these deposits is to discourage imports.)

Still other nontariff barriers may take the form of marking and labeling requirements, "buy national" legislation, and controls or regulations imposed primarily for attaining objectives other than merely keeping imported goods out of the country. A number of other nontariff barriers could be identified if one looked around the world, but because our topic is basically United States import trade it will suffice to examine a few U.S. barriers.

Import Quotas

Quantitative limitations, or quotas, are of two types: tariff rate and absolute. The former provides for the entry of a specified amount of a given product at a basic rate of duty. No limit is placed on the total amount of the product that may be imported, but all imports beyond the lower-rate level will face a higher duty. Actually, tariff-rate quotas, sometimes called nontariff barriers because of their quota feature, should probably not be labeled as such because they are merely limitations on amounts that can enter at certain rates of duty. Any barrier, such as it is, is in the rate of duty.

Absolute quotas, on the other hand, are the most direct and final barrier to imports because they amount to an embargo beyond a stated quantity. They are wicked in effect because they say that no matter how efficient an importer may become in locating low-cost imports or how low a price he may be able to negotiate, only a certain amount will be permitted to enter, and that is all. Beyond that it is a prohibited import. Because of their positive and immediate impact, and their relative ease of imposition (other than keeping competing suppliers satisfied that they have received a fair shake), import quotas are employed by many countries, including the United States.

The quantitative import limitations employed by the United

States can be placed into four principal groupings. First are those imposed under Section 22 of the Agricultural Adjustment Act. Second is the grouping whose rationale is national security, and here reference is to oil import quotas. Under this program, imports of crude oil, unfinished oil, and petroleum products are subject to licensing by the Department of the Interior. This control is considered necessary as a measure of national security. (Effort was made in 1970 to replace oil import quotas with a tariff against imports, but the proposal was defeated.)

A third category is that wherein the products are the subject of international commodity control agreements. The United States was a participant as of mid-1971 in two of these, pertaining to coffee and cotton products.

The fourth grouping of United States quantitative limits on imports includes those against certain dairy and other agricultural products, hard-fiber cordage from the Philippines, and watches and watch movements admissible duty-free from insular possessions of the United States. One should probably add another category, that of "voluntary" export controls employed and enforced by certain other countries, the adoption of which was to avoid threatened mandatory import controls by the United States.

A tabulation of commodities subject to import quotas administered by the commissioner of customs, Treasury Department, is to be found in *Exporting to the United States*, 1969.[2] Other quota controls are administered by other government agencies, specifically the Department of Agriculture, the Department of Commerce, and the Department of the Interior, but actual enforcement, aside from issuing licenses, is effected by the Bureau of Customs because any importation must be processed through its hands.

"Buy American"

Among nontariff trade barriers, one that ranks high is "buy American," or "buy local" legislation or practice. In the United States, the basic legislation is the Buy American Act of 1933. Under it, preference in procurement with public funds must be

---

[2] U.S. Department of the Treasury, Bureau of Customs, *Exporting to the United States*, 1969, p. 63. To bring the table up to early 1971, two items should be added: animal feeds containing milk or milk derivatives, and ice cream.

given to goods of domestic origin unless they are for use outside the United States and its territories, they are not available in sufficient quantity or quality, the head of the agency determines that their purchase would be "inconsistent with the public interest," or he determines their cost to be unreasonable.

In order to bring about some uniformity in applying these directives, the president issued Executive Order 10582, which specifies that the offer of a domestic supplier is to be considered unreasonable if it exceeds the foreign offered price by more than 6 percent, duty-paid and delivered. Exceptions are permitted, raising the permissible differential to 12 percent in cases involving special reasons of national interest, procurement from small businesses, procurement in areas of substantial unemployment, and protection of national security interests. Beyond this, certain exceptions are permitted. The best-known exception probably is that related to balance of payments difficulties, as a result of which the Department of Defense adopted a 50 percent differential in 1962 as a guideline.

The principle of "buy American" was adopted in a number of other pieces of legislation, notably the following:

- A proviso in the annual Defense Appropriations Act (often referred to as the Berry Amendment) that no part of the appropriation shall be available for the purchase of any article of food or clothing not grown or produced in the United States or its possessions, except to the extent that the secretary of the department concerned shall determine that a satisfactory quality and sufficient quantity cannot be procured at U.S. market prices without unduly increasing future U.S. market prices. Certain exceptions are listed, but the discretion is narrower than under the "buy American" legislation.
- The Strategic and Critical Materials Stockpiling Act of 1946, which requires that purchases of strategic and critical materials be made in accordance with provisions of the Buy American Act of 1933.
- The Merchant Marine Act of 1936, which provides that, so far as practicable, only materials of the growth, production, or manufacture of the United States shall be used in ship construction under a construction-differential subsidy.
- A provision in federal housing legislation, which subjects the use of funds made available for carrying out the work of the United States Housing Administration to restrictions under the Buy American Act.

In addition to national policy on this point, a number of states have passed or considered legislation that would reserve to domestic producers purchases made from public funds. Here the question seems to be how far a state can go without interfering with the national government's conduct of foreign policy, specifically in regard to the Constitution's commerce clause (Article 1, Section 8).

Mark-of-Origin Regulations

The foregoing barriers to imports bear on the ability to bring goods into the United States competitively. But another barrier against imports—or at least an economic discouragement to them—is found in provisions concerning marking the merchandise as having a foreign origin.

According to Section 304 (2) of the Tariff Act of 1930, and except as later provided in the Act, every article of foreign origin or its container imported into the United States must be marked in a conspicuous place as legibly, indelibly, and permanently as the nature of the article (or container) will permit, in such manner as to indicate to an ultimate purchaser in the United States the English name of the country of origin of the article. The secretary of the treasury is authorized to permit certain exceptions, and also to determine the character of words and phrases or abbreviations that are acceptable as indicating the country of origin.

Furthermore, the secretary can prescribe any "reasonable method of marking, whether by printing, stenciling, stamping, branding, labeling, or by any other reasonable method, and a conspicuous place on the article (or container) where the marking shall appear." Under this authority, certain regulations (Section 11.8 of *Customs Regulations of the United States*) have been issued.

The principal point to note here is that such marking is or may be an expensive process and one that can only or best be done while an item is in the production process. But at that time it may not be known by the producer where it will be sold, at home or abroad, and if abroad, to what country. Such marking does not seem to serve any economic purpose other than to provide an obstacle to imports. The complexity of laws and regulations cited here should make a potential importer recognize the importance of knowing the rules under which he must play the game and knowing them well enough so that when it is necessary he can instruct his foreign suppliers to do what is required to facilitate entry into the United States.

TECHNICAL IMPORTING PROCEDURES

The dominant agency involved in formal import procedure is the Treasury Department, whose Bureau of Customs administers applicable laws and regulations. The commissioner of customs, located in Washington, is accountable to the secretary of the treasury, and the customs territory of the United States is administratively organized into nine regions, each of which is directed by a regional commissioner. Under these are district directors of customs and port directors of customs. (There are some 250 ports of entry.) However, all merchandise may not enter through every port, and in some cases special facilities must be available through which certain imported products must be processed.

Clearing of merchandise through customs is technical and complicated, and exactness is necessary on invoices, markings, classification, and description. When merchandise enters by vessel, the district customs inspectors seal the vessel's hatches, and the ship's manifests (passenger and cargo lists) must be delivered to customs authorities within 48 hours. Customs officers then supervise the unloading of cargo and passengers, and designate the cases to be taken to the customs appraiser's warehouse for examination and appraisal.

An importer's responsibility begins upon the vessel's arrival because duties accrue at that time and liability for the duties constitutes a personal debt from the importer to the United States. Merchandise imported into the United States is held to be the property of the person to whom it is consigned, and the holder of a bill of lading, duly endorsed, is the person who is authorized to file entry. This may be done either in person or by a qualified representative. Filing must be made at the customhouse within five days, exclusive of Sundays and holidays, after the entry of the importing vessel. If it is not done in the time specified, the goods are stored in a general-order bonded warehouse at the expense of the importer. He must enter them within a year or they are subject to seizure and sale.

Entering Goods Through Customs

Several types of entry can be made, the most significant of which is entry for consumption, for here duty becomes applicable immediately. Entry also can be made for placing the imported merchandise in a warehouse under bond, for transportation in bond to another port of entry or for re-export, or it may be placed in a foreign trade zone. The latter three forms of entry do not call for the immediate deposit or payment of duty because the bond offers assurance that it will be paid when and if the merchandise is entered for consumption from the warehouse or after transportation. A bond is not required on goods placed in foreign trade zones. The principal documents required in order to effect entry are the bill of lading (unless it can be shown that there is none), the commercial invoice or the special customs invoice (for importations on which duty amounts to $500 or more unless exception has been made), and the entry document itself, a treasury form.

In addition, the importer must estimate the amount of duty, pay it, and provide a bond in case it is found to be insufficient. The documents are presented to the customhouse, where they are verified by the collector of customs and where the importer deposits the estimated duty. This point is important to remember: he *deposits the estimated duty.* It is not the final duty until the entry has been "liquidated," that is, until final determination of duty assessment has been made. This may take weeks or months. Meanwhile, the importer must sell at a fixed price and when he does, he can no longer recover any increased duty levied against him. However, he can get from the Customs Bureau an advance ruling or preliminary decision as to classification and duty rate on the basis of a sample of the product intended to be exported.

In the meantime, the goods will be or will have been in the process of examination and appraisal by the customs appraiser, who must satisfy himself as to their classification, the tariff paragraph under which they are listed, the rate of duty applicable, and the value. As stated earlier, value, for duty purposes, is not necessarily the same as invoice value. The value to be used is specified by law.

When merchandise comes into U.S. territory, it becomes subject to other laws, some of which have at times been called nontariff trade barriers. Among these are safety regulations, as were prescribed for automobiles in the late 1960s, and health and sanitary regulations, such as those prescribed by the Food, Drug, and Cosmetics Act. These are not import restrictions by intent, but imports may become casualties on the same basis as domestically produced goods.

Protests and Appeals

If there is agreement between the importer and customs officials, the goods are released, duties are finalized, and the customs entry is liquidated. In case of a dispute as to either classification or appraised value, however, a mechanism of adversary proceedings has been established by which protests and appeals to superior authority may be invoked. In brief, the procedures available are about as shown in the table. (Details of these provisions are covered in Sections 514–516 of Special and Administrative Provisions of the Tariff Act of 1930.)

Action	*By*	*Against*	*Filed with*
Protest	Importer	Decision of appraiser	Collector of customs
Protest	Manufacturer, producer, or wholesaler	Appraised value by customs appraiser: secretary may instruct collector to file appeal for reappraisal. Classification: secretary may instruct collectors.	Secretary of treasury
Appeal	Collector of customs	Decision of appraiser	U.S. Customs Court (one judge)
Appeal	Importer, producer, or collector of customs	Decision of U.S. Customs Court	Court of Customs and Patents Appeals (three judges)

A cursory review of Customs Court decisions in May, June, and July 1969, indicates that about half the decisions were in favor of customs authorities, about 40 percent favored the importer, and 10 percent were partly in favor of one and partly in favor of the other.

Foreign Trade Zones

Among the types of entry by which the government is officially notified of merchandise brought into the United States is one for placing it in a foreign trade zone. Foreign trade zones were authorized by legislation in 1934 as one means of encouraging American foreign commerce.

By primary intent, a foreign trade zone is physically a part of U.S. customs territory but legally it is not, insofar as payment of duty is concerned. In other words, foreign merchandise may be brought into a foreign trade zone without payment of duty, and within the zone the merchandise may be stored, examined, sampled, graded, cleaned, repacked, assembled, processed in other ways, exhibited, sold in wholesale quantities, and manufactured with minimum customs supervision. No duties are paid on it if it is reexported, but regular duties are paid if it enters the American market.

The availability of these facilities makes possible a number of foreign trade opportunities that would not exist otherwise. First is that when bringing foreign merchandise in, not only is no duty paid; not even a bond to cover duty is required. Thus capital outlays for customs duties are deferred until the goods, in whatever form, actually enter U.S. customs territory for consumption. Second, if the goods are later exported, in whatever form and with or without U.S. domestic merchandise content, no duty is payable to the United States. Third, if goods are placed in a foreign trade zone solely for export, they are considered to have been exported for purposes of drawback or bonding.

Foreign trade zones are located in New York, New Orleans, San Francisco, Seattle, Toledo, Honolulu, and Mayagüez, Puerto Rico. A few subzones are in operation or are authorized. In 1969 and 1970 extensive discussions were held over a proposal to establish a zone in Machiasport, Maine, and another in Savannah, Georgia, for the purpose of covering oil refineries desiring to process imported oil that would in some way circumscribe the restrictions of the U.S. oil import program. Hearings were held about the same time on a proposal by the Tariff Commission to abolish foreign trade zones, but as of late 1971 no final action had been taken on either. However, in early 1970 a subzone in Hawaii was authorized for the purpose of processing oil, most of which would be exported but part of which would be sold for use of aircraft and ships in international travel at Honolulu.[3]

The use of foreign trade zones is not free; space must be rented or storage charges must be paid as in any warehouse.

---

[3] *Washington Evening Star*, April 21, 1970.

10

Financing of Exports and Imports: Background and Service Function

International trade involves certain risks not found in domestic trade, notably the surrender of physical control over merchandise and documents during a sometimes long voyage, when the merchandise and evidence of ownership become subject to laws different from those of the exporter; the possibility that collecting the sales price may be subject to foreign legal procedures if arbitration has not been agreed upon and if it becomes advisable or necessary to enforce collection; and that an importer may have to await delivery for a long time after placing an order and the merchandise sent by an exporter may not conform to what the importer expected, or may not be delivered when anticipated.

Because of these considerations, and especially because of the need for exporters and importers to have their interests looked after over long time periods and possibly long distances, the use of documents has evolved as a significant means of determining that someone has either done what is expected of him, or he has not. Because of the important role of documents in credit arrangements, their function in the financing of foreign trade is dominant even though they, themselves, do not provide funds. However, they do facilitate the acquisition of funds.

Importer's Need for Financing

The operational necessity of acquiring merchandise, displaying it until it is sold, and then waiting for payment explains fairly well the need for financing on the part of importers. This is especially true in the light of possibly limited resources of a firm and of seasonal and cyclical characteristics of business. As suggested earlier, an exporter surrenders physical control of merchandise on the strength of his estimate of the importer's willingness and ability to pay.

Exporter's Need for Financing

Aside from the fact that competition and the bargaining position of a buyer (importer) as against that of a seller (exporter) influence terms of sale, a few fundamentals of an exporter's position must be understood. He, too, is enmeshed in a web of *assets, liabilities,* and *time,* perhaps more than an importer.

An exporter always needs cash, either to pay maturing obligations and current running expenses or to replenish merchandise while taking on receivables arising from credit sales. Long-term liabilities eventually become short-term; and short-term obligations are always falling due. But he cannot convert merchandise into cash when receivables are the bottleneck. At the same time, in many cases one cannot sell except on credit, either because competition does so or because a buyer is unable to pay in advance or to arrange other financing.

Risks

The basic risks in international trade fall on an exporter, an importer, or both. Either may have to turn to the banking system if a transaction cannot be financed. Furthermore, it is normal to have recourse to the banking system for the collection of drafts and protection of documents even when the financing is only between the exporter and importer, so it is appropriate to identify these major risks because they influence the types of financial assistance sought and made available. Most basically, the risks are:

1. *The buyer's (importer's) willingness and financial ability to pay.* Closely related to this is his *legal* ability to pay, controlled by his government's policies that may impede payment. In times of exchange difficulties, some countries have importers pay into the central (government-owned) bank (or to other banks under its control) the amount of obligations owed foreign exporters. These accounts may then be frozen, or blocked, leaving the exporter with no legal recourse against the importer.

2. *The seller's (exporter's) willingness and ability to perform according to contract.* Here one runs into obstacles that may be within or beyond an exporter's control. Among the former are conformity to specifications, including delivery data and quality control. Also, an exporter may find himself impeded by happenings beyond his control, such as strikes or undependable shipping schedules—schedules that perhaps were unreasonable to begin with unless everything went like clockwork. This is especially significant in goods with seasonal characteristics.

3. *Exchange-rate fluctuations.* Someone must always stand this and, as indicated earlier, even short-term normal fluctuations are large enough to wipe out net profits on some sales.

4. *In the use of secured credits, physical hazards to the merchandise.* This is not to suggest that protection against physical hazards to merchandise is not important in unsecured credits, but the security arrangement suggests positive reliance on the availability of and realizable value of merchandise in addition to the credit standing and reputation of a borrower.

The risks, then, are rooted in ethical, financial, and physical uncertainties and are more pronounced in foreign than in domestic trade. Accordingly, it is necessary to fix responsibility for these risks by negotiation well in advance of having to lay the burden on someone. Furthermore, it is necessary to have some way of obtaining evidence of performance or nonperformance by an exporter and an importer. Certain trade practices and customs intended to cover some of these nonfinancial risks have evolved and they are an integral part of what is known as financing, *for banks realize that these inherent, additional nonfinancial risks can adversely affect what might otherwise appear as acceptable banking risks.* The financing of international trade is closely linked with the need to insure that each party does what he has promised. It involves more than the mere provision of funds; and this is where documents come into such prominence in international trade financing.

CREDIT TERMS

There are no "required" credit terms, although something close to this may appear from time to time because of foreign government regulations related to foreign exchange controls. It is common to hear reference to "usual," "normal," or "typical" credit terms, but what these adjectives mean is anyone's guess.

Credit terms can be said to depend on or be influenced by the product; the financial condition of the exporter and the importer; economic and political conditions in the foreign market; certain physical, geographic, and legal factors; and what is called "customs of the trade."

Nature of the Product

The product must be surrendered over an extended period. Stoppage of delivery in transit, or recovery and repossession after delivery, may be necessary if, in the meantime, an importer goes bankrupt, becomes slow in paying other creditors or dies, or there is a riot or revolution in his country, and so on. What is to be done with undelivered merchandise, which may be thousands of miles away, may not be an easy decision. The prime considerations are whether the product is perishable, whether it is a staple, and whether it must or can be sold and delivered promptly to another buyer. Another consideration is whether it is a specialty product, one of rather standard usage and acceptability, or one made to order. Another consideration related to the product is the marketing or processing time faced by an importer or buyer, which affects the time within which he can obtain funds with which to pay his obligation to an exporter.

Financial Condition of Exporter and Importer

The individual financial positions of an exporter and importer, and especially the credit standing of an importer, are a major influence in determining the credit terms to be employed. Closely related to this are economic and political conditions in the country of the importer. It may be that delays are being experienced in the collection of drafts, or that the importer's country delays or refuses to make foreign exchange available to pay for trade obligations, or that the country is in a period of recession or depression, or it may be one of the seemingly perpetual victims of inflation, all of which affect an importer's ability to pay, no matter how willing he may be.

Conditions in the Foreign Market

That these conditions frequently change and are under constant attention of exporters is evidenced by the work of the Foreign Credit Interchange Bureau of the National Association of Credit Management in New York. A semiannual survey is made by this bureau, based on questionnaires to manufacturers and exporters located in all parts of the United States and in Europe, covering conditions in each of some 40 foreign countries. For the former, the countries are rated as prompt, fairly prompt, and slow. With respect to estimates on credit conditions, each country is rated as good, fair, or poor. Table 19 summarizes responses for the second half of 1970. In reporting credit terms granted during a half-year as compared with the preceding half-year, respondents indicate that their terms are more liberal, less liberal, or show no change. This exchange of experience and estimates of the various country situations are valuable background knowledge to have in determining the credit conditions or terms to be specified from time to time.

Table 20 reproduces the result of the survey of terms granted

Table 19. Summary of credit conditions reported in 85th semiannual survey of credit conditions for second half of 1970.

Credit Conditions	*Latin America*	*Europe*
Collection experience		
Prompt	5	10
Fairly prompt	16	6
Slow	3	1
Overall credit conditions		
Good	10	11
Fair	10	5
Poor	4	1

SOURCE: *FCIB Bulletin #6111,* National Association of Credit Management, New York, February 12, 1971.

NOTE: Figures represent number of countries.

during the second half of 1970 as compared with the first half. Intelligence on payment records of individual companies abroad is interchanged among exporters and bankers, and suppliers also interchange knowledge among themselves as to the credit terms offered individual buyers.

Table 20. Survey of terms granted during second half of 1970 as compared with the first half of 1970.

	No Change (%)	*More Liberal* (%)	*Less Liberal* (%)
Latin America			
Argentina	79.4	12.9	7.7
Bahamas-Bermuda	95.2	2.4	2.4
Bolivia	48.3	0	51.7
Brazil	69.3	17.8	12.9
Chile	25.6	0	74.4
Colombia	76.9	10.3	12.8
Costa Rica	88.1	2.4	9.5
Dominican Republic	68.3	2.4	29.3
Ecuador	52.2	4.4	43.4
El Salvador	86.7	4.4	8.9
Guatemala	92.9	2.4	4.7
Haiti	72.7	6.1	21.2
Honduras	94.4	0	5.6
Jamaica	90.6	4.7	4.7
Mexico	85.4	6.3	8.3
Nicaragua	94.6	0	5.4
Panama	95.8	2.1	2.1
Paraguay	82.4	0	17.6
Peru	44.2	0	55.8
Puerto Rico	81.1	11.3	7.6
Surinam & N. Antilles	94.0	3.0	3.0
Trinidad & Tobago	91.7	2.7	5.6
Uruguay	71.4	0	28.6
Venezuela	85.7	4.1	10.2
Europe			
Austria	85.7	10.7	3.6
Belgium	87.8	4.9	7.3
Denmark	87.8	7.3	4.9
Finland	96.3	3.7	0
France	82.2	8.9	8.9
Germany (West)	88.6	11.4	0
Greece	79.5	5.1	15.4

Table 20 (Continued)

	No Change (%)	*More Liberal (%)*	*Less Liberal (%)*
Italy	74.4	4.7	20.9
Netherlands	91.3	6.5	2.2
Norway	97.1	2.9	0
Portugal	83.3	10.0	6.7
Spain	86.0	4.7	9.3
Sweden	79.0	13.2	7.8
Switzerland	84.6	12.8	2.6
Turkey	76.2	0	23.8
United Kingdom	76.5	15.7	7.8
Yugoslavia	70.0	15.0	15.0

SOURCE: *FCIB Bulletin #6111,* National Association of Credit Management, New York, February 12, 1971, p. 5.

Physical, Geographic, and Legal Factors

The terms used in credit transactions also are influenced by certain physical, geographic, and legal factors. The time required for transportation is significant. For example, because air freight reduces the time it takes for merchandise to reach an importer, the length of credit terms can be reduced, other things being equal. Similarly, laws and institutions pertaining to the movement of and the care and responsibility for both merchandise and documents play an important role in deciding on credit terms. Laws pertaining to creditor-debtor relationships, and to recovery of merchandise, if necessary, must be considered. Also to be considered is the limitation on lenders.

For example, member banks of the Federal Reserve System are permitted to accept drafts drawn against them if the maturity is no longer than 180 days.[1] Acceptances so created must have a self-liquidating characteristic in order to be eligible for rediscount at the Federal Reserve. The limit here is 90 days, so it becomes evident that this will have some influence on the terms that may effectively be employed.

Terms also differ with the products, some of which move only under what are called medium and long terms. As a means of encouraging commercial banks to look with more favor on export

[1] Federal Reserve Act, Section 13.

paper, the Export-Import Bank of Washington opened a special discount facility in 1966 through which banks could borrow from the Export-Import Bank an amount related to the bank's base-date holding of and increase in holding of nonrecourse exporter paper arising from medium-term export sales credit. This special discount facility clearly makes easier the offering of longer terms by exporters.

Classifying credit terms in any order is a matter of judgment, but the following categorization appears to be workable; it identifies common terms in their order of increasing protection to a seller:

- Consignment shipments.
- Sales made on an open, or current, account basis.
- Sales made on the basis of the seller's being authorized to draw a time draft against the buyer. The draft usually is of the "documentary" type, that is, with documents attached thereto becoming available to the importer upon his *acceptance* of the draft, wherein he promises in writing to pay the amount named at the time stated.
- Sales made on the basis of the seller's being authorized to draw a documentary sight draft against the buyer, with documents to be released upon *payment* of the draft by the importer.
- Sales made against the provision of a bank letter of credit, wherein the bank's standing is substituted for that of a buyer (importer), with the exporter authorized to draw his draft against the bank—the draft being either sight or time, according to the agreement.
- Cash with order, or against the presentation of export documents.

Consignment shipments are not a widely used credit arrangement, but they do serve well in the movement of big-volume items, such as wool or other commodities that move to auctions or other concentrated buyer areas. They are especially appropriate for seasonal products that move to major central markets. They also are found in sample or market-testing shipments, from which orders may be anticipated. A particular point to observe here is that when goods move on consignment, the consignor retains title to the merchandise until it is sold. Conflict may develop as to the consignee's proprietary right in the merchandise, particularly if he should become bankrupt, at which time his apparent or available assets would be taken over to satisfy the creditors. One must assure himself that the law gives full protection to a consignor against failure on the part of a consignee since under consignment, ordinary control but not ownership passes to the consignee (sometimes referred to as buyer), who pays the consignor as the goods are sold.

Sales made against open, or current, account are usual in domestic business in the United States. The sales contract is the legal basis of action, should that become necessary. The practical shortcomings of this kind of account are the lack of precise evidence in the case of having to collect through legal force, and the lack of easily identifiable evidence of an asset in the case of having to use it as a basis for obtaining funds. Credit instruments, by their very existence, make an exporter's own financing easier. Open, or current, account terms are not in wide use internationally for another reason: they do not facilitate the use of the several documents referred to elsewhere. Nevertheless, it is probable that a large part of intercompany international trade is conducted on this basis.

By far, the largest part of foreign trade appears to be financed through the use of drafts, which may be payable at sight or which may convert into acceptances. In the latter case, when drawn on importers or buyers, they are referred to as trade acceptances; when drawn on banks, as bank acceptances.

Extent of Financing by Drafts and Bank Acceptances

Commercial banks are not required to report their issuance of letters of credit, which are only contingent undertakings. But, under regulations prescribed by the Treasury Department, they do report monthly to the Federal Reserve Bank of New York their liabilities to and claims on foreigners.[2] Included in the short-term claims on foreigners payable in dollars are collections outstanding for the bank's own account and for account of the bank's domestic customers. The reporting form does not include a similar column for collections outstanding payable in foreign currencies. These drafts are included in a subcolumn titled "All Other Short-Term Claims on Foreigners." Collections outstanding, by definition, include drafts payable on demand or having a maturity of one year or less. Results of these reports are published in the *Treasury Bulletin;* the amount for November 1970 was $2,313 million.[3] In addition, these banks reported acceptances made for account of foreigners at $3,330 million. A large part of this has been for the

---

[2] Foreign Exchange Form B-2.

[3] *Treasury Bulletin,* January 1971, p. 95.

purpose of financing U.S. exports. In recent years Japan has been an active user of this facility. Japanese banks arrange lines of credit with U.S. banks and use the availability to finance Japanese importers of U.S. goods.

Besides these claims reported by the banking system, short-term claims on foreigners held by nonbanking concerns must also be reported, on a quarterly basis. Therefore the information collected is not as current as that from banks. The amount of such claims reported as of June 1970 was $3,816 million payable in dollars and $348 million payable in foreign currencies.[4] Claims on foreigners reported by nonbanking institutions exclude claims on the reporter's "allied organizations" abroad (interpreted here to mean intercompany accounts between U.S. firms and their affiliates abroad), deposits with banks abroad in the reporter's own name, and claims held for collection by U.S. banks or by the U.S. branch of a foreign bank.

Summarizing liberally these indications of financial practice, one may infer that a rather substantial portion of U.S. exports is financed through the use of drafts entered for collection by the banking system, credits extended directly by exporters, and acceptances made by banks to finance exports. The tabulation for short-term financing is shown in Table 21. If we add to this the long-

Table 21. Indicated export financing practice, November 30, 1970 ($ million).

	Amount
Reported by Banks	
Collections outstanding for own account and for domestic customers (demand to one year)	$2,313 *
Acceptances made by banks to finance exports (from Monthly Acceptance Survey, December 1970)	1,388 †
Reported by Nonbank Institutions	
Short-term claims (excluding deposits with banks abroad, intercompany accounts between U.S. firms and affiliates abroad; and claims held through banks)	3,816 ‡
Total short-term	$7,517

* *Treasury Bulletin,* January 1971, p. 95.
† "Bankers' Acceptance Survey" for December 1970, released by Federal Reserve Bank of New York, January 26, 1971.
‡ *Treasury Bulletin,* January 1971, p. 105 (data for June 1970).

[4] Ibid., p. 105.

term claims of $2,725 million reported by nonbanking concerns, part of which must represent medium- and long-term sales, it becomes apparent that these four methods of financing at, say, an average maturity of even 90 days, represent a large part of total U.S. exports of some $43 billion in 1970.

Interest in knowing more about the method of financing foreign trade has increased because of the close relationship between exports and credit, and because of exhortations, especially by the Department of Commerce and Eximbank, to expand exports as a means of improving the United States balance of payments picture.

THE SERVICE FUNCTION IN FINANCING

A distinction is made between the servicing functions involved in the handling of financial arrangements without the provision of actual funds, and the provision of funds. Included in the former are three major activities that are part and parcel of the financing of exports and imports. These are the collection of drafts, the issuance and use of letters of credit, and the purchase and sale of foreign exchange by banks.

Drafts and Trade Acceptances [5]

Drafts are commonly classified as to tenor (sight or time) and documentary attachments. (Tenor indicates the life of a draft, or the time at which it is to be paid: upon presentation, that is, sight, to the person on whom drawn, or at a later date, that is, time, which must be definitely determinable in order for the draft to qualify as a negotiable instrument.) If payment is called for at a time other than on first presentation, the drawee is expected to accept the draft, signifying his agreement with the amount, manner, time, and place of payment. It then is known as an *acceptance*, and the acceptor is looked on to be ready and willing to pay the obligation at maturity. Drafts facilitate financing by the exporter, for he is then in a better position to pledge, discount, or sell the acceptance and receive his own funds without delay but at the cost of negotiating fees and interest charges.

A further advantage, to both exporters and importers, is the use of documentary drafts. An exporter has assurance that the bank

---

[5] Parts of this section and the next are drawn from Harold J. Heck, *Foreign Commerce* (New York: McGraw-Hill Book Company, Inc., 1953).

that presents a draft for payment or acceptance will not release the documents to the importer until he either pays or accepts, whichever is specified. This retention of control eases the position of the exporter. A documentary draft also offers an importer real advantages because the documents tell him whether certain provisions of the order have been complied with. For example, the bill of lading is evidence that shipment was made by the exporter and indicates whether the merchandise was in apparent good condition when received by the common carrier.

Collection of foreign drafts. Inasmuch as drafts commonly are used in conjunction with documents of title, the function of collecting foreign drafts is of interest to every exporter. A satisfactory arrangement is to collect these drafts through banks, the bank of the drawer forwarding the instrument for collection through its correspondent serving the area of the buyer or drawee.

Instructions to the bank are based in part on selling terms, and the drawer gives detailed advice to the bank as to what to do in case of certain possible developments. Figure 10 illustrates an instruction form that the drawer turns over to his bank with the draft. The drawer's bank passes the same instructions along to its correspondent.

Even for a draft payable on presentation, several weeks may intervene between shipment of merchandise and receipt of payment. The Chase Manhattan Bank publishes a quarterly report of its collection experience for documentary drafts covering U.S. shipments abroad. Table 22 incorporates the results of a random selection from the report for the fourth quarter of 1970. The columns on sight drafts show the time elapsed between the date the documents were airmailed and the date the proceeds were received by the Chase Manhattan Bank. The columns on time drafts show time elapsed between the maturity dates of the drafts and the dates the proceeds were received.

The significance of waiting more than four weeks for receipt of the proceeds from over half the sight drafts collected from 12 of the countries shown, and more than ten weeks for receiving proceeds of some of the sight drafts collected from practically all of the countries shown has particular bearing on the internal financing of an exporter. One should also note, however, that over half the sight drafts paid in 12 of the countries listed yielded remittances within four weeks of airmailing of the documentary drafts for payment.

As stated earlier, it is not known to what extent foreign trade is financed by trade drafts or trade acceptances but evidence sug-

FIGURE 10.
Instruction form for collecting a draft.

THE BANK OF NEW YORK
International Division
P. O. Box 11,210
New York, N. Y. 10049

CUSTOMER FOREIGN COLLECTION LETTER
(Use one form for each collection.)

April 8, 1971

Dear Sirs:

We enclose for collection the undermentioned draft with documents enumerated. Please follow instructions marked "X".

NUMBER	DRAWN ON	TENOR	AMOUNT	STEAMER
				S/S SPEEDQUEEN
EXP	CIA JOHN DOE LA CRUZ, COSTA RICA	Sight	$17,132.54	MERCHANDISE MACHINE PARTS

DRAFTS ORIG.	DRAFTS DUP.	NEGOTIABLE BILLS OF LADING ORIG.	DUP.	TRIP.	NON-NEGO. B/L	CONSULAR INVOICES	INSURANCE CTFS. ORIG.	DUP.	INVOICES ORIG.	DUP.	TRIP.	INSP. CERTIF.	WEIGHT CERTIF.	CERTIF. OF ORIGIN	PARCEL POST RECEIPTS	MISCELLANEOUS
1	1	3/3			4 NN		1	1	1	1	1					

PLEASE TAKE NOTE THAT ALL DOCUMENTS WILL BE AIRMAILED IN ONE MAIL UNLESS OTHERWISE SPECIFICALLY INSTRUCTED BY YOU

[ ] Present on arrival of merchandise
[ ] Deliver Documents on acceptance
[X] Deliver Documents on payment
[ ] Protest for non-acceptance
[X] Protest for non-payment
[ ] Do not protest

Advise by [X] Air Mail / [ ] Cable — [ ] Non-acceptance, [X] Non-payment, [ ] Acceptance, [X] Payment

[ ] Payable at collecting bank's selling rate for Air Mail checks on New York, on date of payment, remitting proceeds by Air Mail.
[ ] Interest to be collected at % from date of issue until approximate arrival of cover in New York.
[ ] Interest to be collected at % per annum for any delay in payment.
[ ] Allow drawee discount at % per annum for anticipated payment on if paid at
[ ] In the event U. S. Dollar cover is not immediately obtainable, a provisional deposit in local currency may be accepted under drawees' written obligation to assume all exchange risks.
[ ] Remit proceeds by cable, difference between check and cable funds and cable expenses for our account.

[ ] Incur no cable expense
[X] Foreign bank charges — [X] Drawee's expense [ ] Drawer's expense
[X] Your charges — [X] Drawee's expense [ ] Drawer's expense
[ ] Do not waive charges
[X] Waive charges if refused by drawee
[X] In case of need, refer to

JOHN SMITH
NAME

LA CRUZ, COSTA RICA
ADDRESS

who is authorized

[X] Only to obtain honoring of draft as drawn
[ ] To give instructions which may be followed in every respect

[X] Special Instructions

Please arrange to present the documents through:
The Drawee Bank
La Cruz, Costa Rica

It is understood and agreed that, having exercised due care in the selection of any correspondent to whom the above mentioned item may be sent for collection you shall not be responsible for any act, omission, default suspension, insolvency or bankruptcy of any such correspondent or its sub-agent, or for any delay in remittance, loss in exchange or loss of said items or their proceeds during transmission or in any course of collection.

Very truly yours,

PARTS EXPORT, INC. NEW YORK
(FIRM OR CORPORATION)

(AUTHORIZED SIGNATURE REQUIRED)

Remit proceeds to us by [ ] Check [X] Crediting our account # 139-53

1-2-07-126 (8-70)

Except as otherwise specifically stated herein, this transaction is subject to 'Uniform Rules for the Collection of Commercial Paper' - I C C Brochure #254

Table 22. Chase Manhattan Bank experience in collecting documentary drafts of U.S. exports, (4th quarter 1970).

	Percentage of Sight Drafts Paid				*Percentage of Time Drafts Paid*			
Country	*In 4 Weeks*	*In 5–10 Weeks*	*In 11–15 Weeks*	*In 16 Weeks and Over*	*In 4 Weeks*	*In 5–10 Weeks*	*In 11–15 Weeks*	*In 16 Weeks and Over*
Argentina	39	55	4	2	80	10	5	5
Australia	71	27	2	—	85	11	4	—
Belgium	62	29	6	3	65	28	2	5
Brazil	53	39	7	1	63	24	7	6
Colombia	5	30	30	35	28	22	22	28
El Salvador	30	54	12	4	64	26	8	2
France	40	44	12	4	71	21	5	3
Germany	57	39	3	1	45	18	14	23
Greece	33	56	8	3	46	38	8	8
Japan	39	50	6	5	66	14	15	5
Mexico	55	34	5	6	52	27	10	11
Netherlands	78	18	3	1	80	18	2	—
Panama	63	32	3	2	58	26	6	10
Peru	40	42	13	5	51	24	8	17
Spain	36	46	7	11	72	5	18	5
Sweden	77	21	1	1	93	6	1	—
Switzerland	74	20	3	3	64	7	9	20
United Kingdom	81	16	3	—	70	22	7	1
Venezuela	55	32	9	4	65	22	7	6

SOURCE: Chase Manhattan Bank, *Guide for Exporters*, December 31, 1970.

gests that this is perhaps the method used in arranging payment for the greatest volume of trade.

Another indication of the role played by bank acceptances may be had by relating the total of bank acceptances outstanding, when adjusted to an annual estimate of volume by assuming an average life of 90 days, to reported export and import volumes. The computation suggests that in 1970 as much as 15 percent of exports and 25 percent of imports of merchandise were financed by bank acceptances. It should be noted, though, that this figure is of *acceptances,* and that sight credits by banks, under letters of credit, are not included. Accordingly, the proportion of foreign trade financed by means of bank letters of credit (both sight and time arrangements) would be substantially larger than the percentages indicated for acceptances alone.

Issuance and Use of Letters of Credit

These instruments are letter forms issued by a bank authorizing the beneficiary to draw on it or on some other bank with which arrangements have been made and signifying the bank's commitment to honor drafts if drawn under the conditions stipulated in the letter of credit.

Terms to be complied with are those specified by the party requesting the bank to open the letter of credit. They must, of course, be agreeable to both the seller and the buyer. It is primarily the seller's uncertainty as to the buyer's ability or willingness to pay that compels him to ask the buyer to cover the transaction by a bank letter of credit. In doing so, the personal phase of credit risk to an exporter is practically eliminated. But the credit must be one the seller can live with, for he then runs the risk of not performing as specified before expiration of the credit. In addition, the seller may desire this type of credit because it makes his own financing arrangements easier. He then has the right to draw a draft on a bank whose reputation is known, and he therefore has a more marketable asset when he needs to raise funds for his own operations.

Advantages to both importer and exporter. There are other advantages, to both seller and buyer, in the use of bank letters of credit. For the seller, if the draft is to be in a foreign currency, the high standing of a reputable bank as drawee, regardless of currency denomination, makes it easier for him to dispose of it. As in the case of collecting drafts through banks, the seller obtains protection by reserving documents of title in his effective possession until the draft has been accepted by a bank satisfactory to him. In this connection there is an added advantage, in that before negotiating the draft the bank will check the documents carefully to be sure that all specified conditions of the letter of credit have been complied with.

Although a letter of credit is an expense, a buyer will also find advantages in using this type of financing. It is the equivalent of a source of funds to him, just as a direct loan from a bank would be, and the total cost may be less than that of a direct loan. Other benefits also accrue. With the credit risk reduced or practically eliminated, the buyer is in a position to obtain more favorable price consideration. Since the bank makes a check of documents against specifications, the buyer's interest is protected. If the seller fails to conform to the points specified in the letter of credit, the buyer is under no obligation. Thus, a seller's malpractices or mistakes are screened as a protection to the buyer. These malpractices and mistakes may relate to such aspects as time of shipment, quality of goods, quantity of goods, packing, insurance, and marking. However, none of the seller's or buyer's responsibility is placed on the bank. The bank pays off on documents only, as stated earlier. There is, furthermore, an advantage to the bank in that it is not lending funds but is lending its name only.

Revocable and irrevocable credits. A letter of credit may be revocable or irrevocable. The former reserves to the issuing bank the right to revoke the credit at any time before negotiation, without prior notice to the beneficiary. Accordingly, use of this type is restricted to circumstances wherein the exporter and importer have some other satisfactory basis for proceeding with the business at hand. An irrevocable credit is a firm commitment by the issuing bank for the period specified in the letter of credit. During the life of the credit, it cannot be canceled or modified to the detriment of the beneficiary without the agreement of all parties concerned. This gives an exporter greater protection because the importer cannot decide to cancel, reduce, or modify the order to the disadvantage of the exporter, who looks to the bank to pay or accept the draft drawn under terms of the credit regardless of the bank's relationship to the importer. Figure 11 illustrates an irrevocable letter of credit.

Confirmed and unconfirmed credits. Another significant differentiation in letters of credit is that between *unconfirmed* and *confirmed*. The former refers to a credit opened by a foreign bank in favor of an exporter, with notification given to the exporter by a bank in his own country, but without that bank's assuming obliga-

FIGURE 11.
Irrevocable letter of credit.

THE BANK OF NEW YORK

48 WALL STREET, NEW YORK, N. Y. 10015

April 8, 1971

IRREVOCABLE
LETTER OF CREDIT
No. 21043

R. Verdes Enterprises
32 Manila Street
Djakarta, Indonesia

DEAR SIRS:

WE HEREBY AUTHORIZE YOU TO VALUE ON THE BANK OF NEW YORK, NEW YORK, N. Y.

FOR ACCOUNT OF M. Clarke Trading., No. 1 Control Lane, New York, N. Y.
UP TO THE AGGREGATE AMOUNT OF ONE HUNDRED TWENTY SIX THOUSAND AND 00/100 DOLLARS ($126,000.00) U.S. CURRENCY
AVAILABLE BY YOUR DRAFTS AT sight, accompanied by:

Commercial invoice in triplicate, indicating that the merchandise is in accordance with Contract No(s) 3176.

Signed Weight Notes in triplicate.

Full set, clean on-board ocean bills of lading, showing the beneficiary as shipper for and on behalf of the INDONESIAN BANK through which the draft and documents are negotiated, consigned to the order of the NEGOTIATING BANK, and endorsed by that bank to the order of THE BANK OF NEW YORK, marked:"Notify M. Clarke Trading., No. 1 Control Lane, New York, N. Y.", and "FREIGHT COLLECT", dated not later than November 15, 1971.

EVIDENCING SHIPMENT OF: ABOUT ONE HUNDRED (100) TONS CRUDE RUBBER. F.O.B. Djakarta, Indonesia. From Djakarta, Indonesia to U.S.A. Port. Partial shipments permitted.

On-board bills of lading issued by the ocean carrying vessel destined as stated, or through bills of lading endorsed on-board by the ocean carrying vessel destined as stated are required. Either the date of the on-board ocean bills of lading, or the date of the through bills of lading constitutes date of shipment.

The negotiating bank's certificate that a full set of bills of lading has been received and endorsed by them to the order of THE BANK OF NEW YORK, must also accompany the draft and documents.

All banking charges outside The United States are for your account.

Insurance, marine and war risks, will be effected by buyer.

DRAFTS MUST BE DRAWN AND NEGOTIATED NOT LATER THAN December 31, 1971.

ALL DRAFTS DRAWN UNDER THIS CREDIT MUST BEAR ON THEIR FACE THE CLAUSE "DRAWN UNDER THE BANK OF NEW YORK CREDIT NO. 21043 ." AND THE AMOUNT OF ANY DRAFT DRAWN UNDER THIS CREDIT MUST BE ENDORSED ON THE REVERSE HEREOF BY THE NEGOTIATING BANK.

EXCEPT SO FAR AS OTHERWISE EXPRESSLY STATED, THIS CREDIT IS SUBJECT TO THE UNIFORM CUSTOMS AND PRACTICE FOR DOCUMENTARY CREDITS (1962 REVISION) INTERNATIONAL CHAMBER OF COMMERCE, BROCHURE NO. 222.

WE HEREBY AGREE WITH THE DRAWERS, ENDORSERS AND BONA FIDE HOLDERS OF DRAFTS DRAWN IN COMPLIANCE WITH THE TERMS OF THIS CREDIT, THAT THE SAME SHALL BE DULY HONORED ON PRESENTATION TO THE DRAWEE.

YOURS VERY TRULY.

AUTHORIZED SIGNATURE

tion or responsibility. It will clarify the discussion if we assume the exporter to be in the United States.

Advice to the exporter (by the United States bank) that such a credit has been opened is usually accompanied by a clause reading more or less as follows: "This advice conveys no engagement on our part and is simply for your guidance in preparing and presenting drafts and documents." It may be of interest to note that even though the exporter is authorized to draw his draft on a bank in the United States, the bank assumes no formal responsibility to pay or accept the draft.

A confirmed letter of credit, on the other hand, carries with it a definite commitment on the part of a bank in the United States. It is therefore more desirable. A confirmed letter of credit is shown in Figure 12, the last sentence of which reads: "We hereby confirm the above credit and undertake that all drafts drawn and presented as above specified will be duly honored by us." Only irrevocable credits are confirmed, and the designations "confirmed" and "unconfirmed" pertain solely to credits opened by other banks. As Figure 12 shows, provision is made for specifying that certain documents be attached to the draft. Under sponsorship of the International Chamber of Commerce a study was undertaken by banks in the major trading countries looking toward the development of a standard uniform letter of credit format for recommended usage by banks on a worldwide basis. As of early 1971 a finalized form was being studied for use by individual banks in the United States.

Purchase and Sale of Foreign Exchange

"Foreign exchange" is the term used to refer to the currencies of other countries in terms of any single one. To a person with United States funds, the pound, franc, and peso are foreign exchange. To the British, the dollar, franc, and peso are foreign exchange. The term is also commonly used to refer to some instruments used in international commerce, such as bills of exchange and bank drafts. They are called pieces of foreign exchange.

In form, foreign exchange may be currency, either paper or metallic, that people carry in their pockets. But by far the greater amount is in the form of drafts drawn by sellers on buyers, by creditors on debtors, by banks on other banks (including checks), and by sellers or creditors on banks.

Because quotations and payments on U.S. import and export transactions may be in U.S. dollars or any foreign exchange, and because commerce between other countries may be quoted and

FIGURE 12.
Confirmed letter of credit.

THE BANK OF NEW YORK

48 WALL STREET, NEW YORK, N. Y. 10015

INTERNATIONAL DEPARTMENT March 26, 1971

OUR ADVICE NO. 40780

MENTION THIS ADVICE NUMBER AND DATE ON ALL DRAFTS AND COMMUNICATIONS

Steel Frames Industries Inc.
4 Labor Lane
Long Island City, New York.

DEAR SIRS:
WE ARE INSTRUCTED BY BANCO VERDES & IRMAOS, LISBON, PORTUGAL

IN THEIR letter OF March 12, 1971 TO ADVISE YOU THAT THEY HAVE OPENED THEIR IRREVOCABLE LETTER OF CREDIT NO. CA26095 FOR A SUM OR SUMS NOT EXCEEDING A TOTAL OF THREE HUNDRED THOUSAND AND 00/100 DOLLARS ($300,000.00) U.S. CURRENCY

FOR ACCOUNT OF Structura Inc., Lisbon, Portugal
AVAILABLE BY YOUR DRAFTS ON US AT sight
ACCOMPANIED BY

Commercial Invoice in sextuplicate, indicating origin of goods, and visaed by a Chamber of Commerce.
Marine Insurance Policy or Certificate.
Full set, clean "on board" Ocean Bills of Lading, consigned to the order of Banco Verdes & Irmaos, Lisbon, Portugal, marked: "Notify Structura Inc., Lisbon, Portugal", and "FREIGHT PAID", dated not later than December 1, 1971.

EVIDENCING SHIPMENT OF: STEEL BARS AND FRAMES. From U.S.A. Port to C.I.F. Lisbon. Partial shipments permitted. Transhipment not permitted.

ALL DRAFTS, WITH DOCUMENTS AS SPECIFIED, MUST BE PRESENTED AT THIS OFFICE NOT LATER THAN December 15, 1971

EXCEPT SO FAR AS OTHERWISE EXPRESSLY STATED, THIS CREDIT IS SUBJECT TO THE UNIFORM CUSTOMS AND PRACTICE FOR DOCUMENTARY CREDITS (1962 REVISION) INTERNATIONAL CHAMBER OF COMMERCE, BROCHURE NO. 222.

THE ABOVE MENTIONED CORRESPONDENT ENGAGES WITH YOU THAT ALL DRAFTS DRAWN UNDER AND IN COMPLIANCE WITH THE TERMS OF THIS ADVICE WILL BE DULY HONORED ON PRESENTATION.

• We hereby confirm the above credit and undertake that all drafts drawn and presented as above specified will be duly honored by us.

YOURS VERY TRULY.

AUTHORIZED SIGNATURE

settled in their own or foreign currencies, including U.S. dollars, many sellers come into possession of foreign exchange that they do not intend to use as money, and many buyers need foreign exchange that they do not possess. This supply of and demand for foreign exchange provides the essentials of a market or, more accurately, several markets in foreign exchange.

Markets can be said to exist in spot (cable or mail) transfers and in futures, in point of time of delivery. But with regard to facilities, there is no formal, central, organized market in the United States except for future contracts in six foreign currencies (British pounds sterling, Deutsche marks, French francs, Italian lire, Japanese yen, and Swiss francs). Contracts in these are traded on the International Commercial Exchange, Inc. This facility began operating in New York in 1970.

Commercial banks serve as marketplace. The principal market facilities for foreign exchange consist of the commercial banks, supplemented by central banks and foreign exchange brokers and dealers. Not all commercial banks are to be included, of course, but many of the larger ones operate branches abroad or maintain balances in one or more foreign countries. Balances are built up by the purchase of drafts or claims payable abroad and are reduced by the sale of such funds to purchasers or debtors in need of them. Thus, foreign exchange is looked on as a commodity, or inventory, to be accumulated and bid up in price, if demand so suggests, or to be reduced in individual holdings and driven down in price when alternative uses for dollars or lessened demand for any one or all types of foreign exchange appear to be the order of the day.

Because each individual bank faces the daily problem of maintaining its "position" in the several foreign currencies by building up or reducing its holdings of each, it follows that the price any bank is willing to pay for, say, British pounds will be influenced not only by general market conditions but by the bank's own specific position on that date. Hence, the effective price for foreign exchange is a matter of determination at a particular moment, taking into consideration such other variables as the type of foreign exchange instrument offered or sought, the amount involved, and the customer's relationship with the bank. Accordingly, buyers and sellers may at times find it advantageous to go to different banks to find the most favorable rate at a particular time.

The New York foreign exchange market has for years consisted of an informal working relationship among major commercial banks and foreign exchange brokers and dealers, with active participation by the Federal Reserve Bank of New York since 1962.

Provision of Credit and Economic Intelligence

Prior to the appearance of a draft or even the making of an export sale on which a draft is based, a substantial amount of commercial intelligence is required, especially by the exporter. Such intelligence will relate to individual firms in other countries and to economic conditions in these countries as well as in the economic sector involved.

One of the most important sources of current intelligence of this type is one's bank, especially if it is large enough and active enough to have international interests. This may be by way of foreign branches or affiliates or by way of correspondent relationships. In the former case, the number of countries on which fullest expertise is maintained will be small; in the latter they may be more. Some banks specialize, one may say, in a few countries or a region, and some publish reports or other material on the countries on which they have most current information.

Because of correspondent linkages, however, most banks are in a position to obtain from correspondents up-to-date intelligence concerning firms and business conditions in practically any part of the world, and this facility, available to the bank's customers, must be looked on as one of the major service functions in the financing of international trade. It influences credit terms, price quotations, and currency quotations, without which there would be fewer sales, fewer drafts to be collected, fewer letters of credit to be issued, and little foreign exchange to be bought and sold.

11

Financing of Exports and Imports: The Provision of Funds

The credit terms outlined in the preceding chapter are listed in order of increasing protection to the seller. They also identify the actual provider of funds for the particular transaction, assuming that an exporter has not yet discounted or otherwise disposed of the asset he obtained through the sale of merchandise to some other provider of funds.

For the first four, and possibly five, identified terms the seller is the source of funds, and the asset financed is merchandise, in the case of shipments on consignment, or receivables, either on open account or evidenced by the authorized use of drafts as long as the drafts remain in the exporter's possession. Where an exporter obtains his funds to carry these assets is beside the point—it may be from his own invested net worth, it may be from a bank loan not immediately related to any specific transaction, or it may be from accounts payable to trade creditors. However, the use of documentary drafts does lend an element of creditor, or exporter, protection because documents attached to the draft are effectively retained under an exporter's control (via the bank collection mechanism) until the buyer pays or accepts the obligation by promising in writing to pay the draft at the agreed date. This evidentiary creation not only clarifies publicly the understanding about the buyer's obligation to pay; it provides an exporter with something he can use to raise funds, if necessary, by discounting the draft/acceptance with his bank.

But a manufacturing exporter will normally not be selling only to foreign buyers and, in fact, exports may be only a small part of his total sales. He may, therefore, be expected to obtain working funds from his bank based on the existence of or secured by such assets as receivables due from either foreign or domestic buyers, or inventory, or other assets. Or the direct loans may be unsecured. More usually, however, an exporter will often discount his draft with his bank at the time it is entered for collection if payable or to be accepted abroad, or accepted by the bank in his country in the case of a time draft. The discounting may be with or without recourse to the exporter. In any of these cases, the bank is the ultimate provider of funds. The exporter may also be in a position to discount the acceptance in a number of places that may be said to constitute a "market."

Bank letters of credit do not, in and of themselves, provide funds, since an exporter, as beneficiary under a letter of credit, and as drawer of the draft on the bank designated in the letter of credit, could hold the draft to maturity (thereby saving the discount fee). At maturity, either sight or after the prearranged time, the bank pays and obviously becomes an actual provider of funds. But until maturity of the draft, an exporter simply possesses the obligation of a bank rather than that of the foreign buyer, and whether or how the importer pays the bank is of small concern to the seller. Bank letters of credit covering exports are based on importer requests, direct or through a foreign bank, or on letters of commitment issued by certain governmental and intergovernmental agencies.

Factoring

A postwar phenomenon in the financing of foreign trade by commercial banks is the appearance of a factoring mechanism. This is a facility that seems to have been first emphasized by the First National Bank of Boston but is now available through a few more banks. Factoring particularly helps credit checking and collection abroad by establishment of a network of banks joined for that purpose, and it is claimed that the arrangement permits more liberal credit terms and faster decisions on orders than would otherwise be possible. Furthermore, the competitive drive for exports has led buyers to demand trade credit on open terms. Approval of the credit by a factor (or his representative) in a foreign country facilitates acceptance of the order and establishment of the receivable. Again, this does not in itself actually provide funds. If advances against the accounts receivable are desired by the exporter, he pays interest for the advance over and above the modest service fee he pays for the factoring. Collection of the receivables is undertaken by the factor in the buyer's own country, and the buyer is normally instructed by invoice to pay the factor.

Special Financing Arrangements Applicable to Imports

In the earlier discussion concerning letters of credit it was pointed out that a bank's credit is substituted for that of a business; in other words, the beneficiary under a letter of credit looks to the bank authorizing him to draw a draft against it to make good on its promise. Furthermore, in considering an importer's need for financing it was stated that he needs merchandise—to sell, to process for sale or to consume in production. But a bank needs assurance that its interest (and that of its depositors) is amply protected, with legal security at times. These aspects of international trade financing stand out more in the financing of imports than of exports, especially the security features.

In American import practice the issuing bank on import credits is usually an American bank, of which the importer is a customer. The bank, which must be paid by the importer, is able to cover its position by the use of two rather standard documents:

A letter of credit application, which must be signed by the importer and must specify the exact conditions to be included in the letter of credit. This application incorporates the particular details of the contract between the buyer (importer) and seller.

A letter of credit agreement, in which the importer acknowledges his evolving indebtedness to the bank and in which he promises (as in a promissory note) to put the bank in funds one day before the draft (or acceptance) falls due.

Then, when the merchandise arrives, it frequently is consigned to order of the bank, which thereby holds effective title, and the importer obtains possession of it in accordance with the arrangement made with his bank. The merchandise could, of course, be released to the importer without specific legal protection of the bank's interest in it. The more normal arrangement, however, is for the bank to release the financed merchandise to the importer upon his execution of a trust receipt or some similar form of security agreement designed to protect the bank's security interest in the collateral. The arrangements provided for in the Uniform Commercial Code have simplified the technical steps involved in protecting and perfecting a security interest; under section 9-202 of the Code, title to the collateral is immaterial. However, the security interest must be properly filed for public notice in order the protect it against claims on or seizure of the collateral by third parties.

This not only provides the legal security that is called for at times in order to make it possible for a bank to create an acceptance, as when legal limitations on credits to one borrower are a limiting factor. It also facilitates the importer's business operations. If the bank consents, as is common practice, the importer may sell or otherwise dispose of the collateral. After all, it is through such transactions that he expects to come into possession of funds with which to pay the bank. In exchange, the importer extends the bank's security interest to the proceeds arising from transactions in the financed merchandise; in effect, he agrees to turn over to the bank the accounts or notes receivable arising from, or cash received from, them.

Schematically, letter of credit origin and processing can be pictured as in Figure 13, which is a modification of the basic pattern of a flow chart. It includes, as will be seen, only the more usual documents. The term "seller's bank" is not intended to mean necessarily the bank with which the seller does most of his banking and financing. It could be that an exporter requests that the letter of credit be negotiated or confirmed or issued by a *named* bank in the United States, but this is normally not the case; the letter of credit will flow through the foreign importer's bank's branch or through a correspondent in the exporter's country.

FIGURE 13.

Origin and processing pattern of letter of credit.

1. Seller offers on Letter of Credit terms.
2. Buyer accepts offer and sales contract is entered.

3. Buyer (Importer)

Applies for Letter of Credit.

Signs Letter of Credit Agreement.

4. Buyer's Bank

(a) Issues Letter of Credit, or

(b) Arranges for another bank to issue.

5. Seller's (Exporter's) Bank (Bank in Exporter's Country)

(a) Negotiates Letter of Credit by buyer's bank if unconfirmed.

(b) Confirms Letter of Credit by buyer's bank if called for.

(c) Issues Letter of Credit if requested to do so by buyer's bank.

In any case, notifies exporter of receipt of Letter of Credit and/or sends to him.

6. Exporter

(a) Examines Letter of Credit to see that it is as called for, and that he can comply with its conditions.

(b) Proceeds to do what is required.

(1) Prepares merchandise for shipment.

(2) Prepares documents called for in Letter of Credit.

(3) Draws draft on bank so authorizing and presents to bank with required documents.

7. Examines documents and draft. If in order, honors draft (pays or accepts). Separates draft from documents and pays exporter or gives him accepted draft (banker's acceptance); forwards documents to importer's bank.

Certificates
Insurance
Invoice
Bill of Lading
Draft

To buyer's bank. → To buyer (importer) under previously arranged conditions. → Buyer obtains goods and pays his bank when due.

Exporter receives cash or acceptance; if the latter, he may hold to maturity, or discount in market. (Bankers acceptances meeting required conditions are eligible for rediscount with or purchase by Federal Reserve Banks.)

FUNDS PROVIDED BY GOVERNMENT BODIES

Most of the preceding discussion of financing of foreign trade was from a microeconomic viewpoint. It presumed that funds would be available or could be made available if the price were right. But a fundamental consideration would be overlooked if it were assumed that the banking system is always sufficiently liquid to meet any demands placed on it to finance exports, or that the banking system will favor exports over domestic business. Because of balance of payments implications and economic development pressures, certain institutions have been established whose business it is to provide funds to facilitate or expand American exports and aid other countries in their economic development plans and programs. The principal institutions, for this subject, are the Export-Import Bank and the Agency for International Development (AID), both of which are U.S. government institutions, and the World Bank Group, which is internationally owned and not specifically concerned with U.S. exports.

Export-Import Bank

An indication of the importance of the Export-Import Bank as a provider of funds to finance exports is its overall lending authority. As of early 1971, this was $13.5 billion in loans, guarantees, and insurance, with guarantees and insurance limited to a total of $3.5 billion.

Eximbank makes long-term loans to public and private borrowers abroad for the purchase of American goods and services for use outside the United States. This is a direct provision of funds to finance foreign trade, especially exports. In addition to providing such funds, the Eximbank encourages commercial banks to make available their own funds for exports through its guarantees to commercial banks and its rediscount facility for commercial banks; and it encourages nonbanking concerns to make their funds more fully available for financing exports through its important role in the Foreign Credit Insurance Association (FCIA).

Commodity Credit Corporation, Department of Agriculture

Although emphasis on organizational and procedural aspects of international trade has been on manufactures, a sizable proportion of American exports consists of agricultural products. Some of these have been the object of special promotional and financial arrangements, one being the purchase of nonconvertible currencies earned through approved exports under Public Law 480. In recent years, however, the objective has shifted toward a goal of dollar financing instead of local currency sales, that is, sales made abroad and calling for payment in U.S. dollars. To facilitate these sales, longer credit terms are frequently required of the exporter and it is to provide this accommodation that funds are made available to exporters by the Commodity Credit Corporation (CCC).

Sales may thus be made abroad by the exporter on longer than usual payment terms (the maximum is three years) and the obligation of the foreign buyer may be assigned and sold to the CCC by the exporter, who receives his funds at the time he completes his contracted responsibility. To effect these transactions, the foreign importer's obligation must be supported by an irrevocable letter of credit in favor of the CCC and issued by an acceptable foreign or United States bank, and the exporter must turn over to the CCC an on-board bill of lading covering the shipment. The CCC then holds the letter of credit and draws on the issuing bank according to the specified maturity date.

Only certain commodities are eligible for this type of financing; the list is published each month by the Export Marketing Service of the Department of Agriculture.

Agency for International Development (AID)

The AID administers the U.S. foreign assistance program, a large part of which consists of providing funds in the form of development loans. AID development loans are usually to foreign governments or their agencies, although in some instances they may be made to private enterprises. In any case, these are the funds foreign buyers use to pay for American exports.

The mechanics are simply that letters of commitment to designated American banks form the basis for such banks' issuing letters of credit in favor of American exporters; the exporter draws his draft, authorized by the letter of credit, and thereby obtains funds provided by an agency of the U.S. government.

International Organizations

The several international lending institutions, to which the United States is a principal contributor, are institutions through which funds are provided to finance imports, which are some other country's exports. Loans for specific projects are made to borrowers abroad who can then shop around and buy to their best advantage, wherever they choose. Insofar as providing funds to American exporters is concerned, the mechanism is substantially via letter of commitment to a bank, its issuance of a letter of credit to the American exporter, and his drawing a draft according to the terms of the credit.

Principal among international organizations providing funds to cover exports (not only from the United States) are the International Bank for Reconstruction and Development (IBRD, or World Bank), the International Development Association, the International Finance Corporation, and regional institutions such as the Inter-American Development Bank and the Asian Development Bank.

EXPORT CREDIT INSURANCE

Not many companies are in a position to allocate their invested resources in the carrying of a large volume of debtor obligations arising from export sales. These receivables may be seasonal or cyclical in volume or relatively long-term in actual collection experience, even though on paper they were initially scheduled as short-term and self-liquidating.

In addition, many products are sold, and can only be sold, on the basis of credit as well as on price. So when an American exporter loses a sale because he finds that his German or Japanese or British competitor offers easier credit terms, he naturally feels he should be in the same position as his competition. This holds especially when the position is "designed" by or influenced by his competitors' governments. Hence there is pressure on the United States government to do something to help its exporters become more competitive in credit terms. The exporter says he cannot do it alone. Yet, without offering credit, and thereby carrying receivables, he cannot compete.

Until 1962, there was no export credit insurance program in the United States, although systems existed in practically all its competitors and most of these were government-supported. Mounting pressure and interest in the formation of an American system resulted in the formation of the Foreign Credit Insurance Association in October 1961, with headquarters in New York.

The FCIA is an unincorporated group of about 50 private insurance companies, operating in partnership with the Export-Import Bank of the United States. It is thus a joint business and government association, established to provide various types of credit insurance to American exporters. This is expected to enable exporters to offer more competitive terms to foreign buyers through being, themselves, better able to obtain financing to carry the receivables. Credit insurance does not, however, relate to the rate of interest charged on credit sales, which could be a significant factor in one's competitive posture at times.

Risks Covered by Insurance

The risks that are the subject of credit insurance may be classified in two ways, according to nature and duration:

Nature. Commercial and political. Commercial risk coverage offers protection against insolvency of or protracted default in payment by the foreign buyer. Political risk coverage is against currency inconvertibility, cancellation or restriction of import or export licenses, expropriation or confiscation, loss due to war, revolution, or civil disturbance, and certain other losses.

Duration. Short- or medium-term. Short-term is considered as up to 180 days; medium-term is from 181 days to five years.

It has been arranged that the Export-Import Bank, which is owned 100 percent by the United States government, assume coverage of the political risks, whereas private insurance companies provide coverage against commercial risks. All risks cannot be eliminated, without some recourse to the exporter, nor should they be. He must be kept "honest," so to speak, by retaining a stake in the final payment. Moreover, risks absorbed by the FCIA must be actuarially sound. Otherwise, the premium rates would be too high.

These considerations have resulted in the adoption of a number of underwriting principles in the insurance operation, which include:

1. Foreign buyers must be credit-worthy, whether business firms, government bodies or, in some cases, individuals.

2. Certain obligations rest with an insured exporter, rendering his credit procedures substantially as they would be without insurance. This has to do with checking of the credit risk and taking steps to prevent loss, such as with overdue accounts or with extensions of time on accounts. In addition, an insured exporter is charged with reporting of slow accounts to the insurer and with transmitting detrimental knowledge concerning a foreign buyer to the insurer.

3. A whole-turnover requirement for short-term credits. Under this specification an exporter must expect to pay premiums (thereby take insurance) on all his short-term export credit sales, with certain optional exclusions, such as those covered by a bank letter of credit, sales to subsidiaries abroad, and sales to Canada.

4. Specific risk coverage related to medium-term credit sales may be negotiated on a case-by-case basis. Generally these are on nonrepetitive, at least not frequently repetitive, sales of high-unit value.

5. In order to facilitate order processing an exporter may negotiate discretionary credit limits with his insurer within which transactions may be qualified for insurance coverage by the exporter under specified criteria without his having to submit a special application in each case.

6. When the contingency arises for settlement of loss claims, the insured must be prepared to submit proof of loss. Moreover, on settlements of less than 100 percent of the amount due, the insurer's approval must be obtained in advance.

7. On losses related to the nonconvertibility, or transfer, element of political risk coverage, the insured must be prepared to submit evidence that the foreign debtor has deposited the amount due in local currency with his country's authorities and that the delay in payment is due to foreign government action.

Eligibility Criteria

The object of the credit insurance program is to assist in increasing American commercial exports. To qualify for short-term insurance coverage, a product must contain at least 50 percent material and labor of U.S. origin and be sold abroad for dollars. However, provision has been made whereby sales in terms of foreign currencies could be eligible for coverage under certain circumstances. To be eligible for medium-term coverage, the goods (generally equipment and other durables and agricultural products) must be produced in the United States and sold abroad for dollars.

Extent of Coverage

For many years up to early 1971, an exporter obtaining insurance against his eligible short-term credit risks could be covered for up to 90 percent of losses arising from commercial risks and up to 95 percent of losses caused by political risks. For medium-term credits, the coverage was up to 90 percent of the financed portion of the contract for losses attributable to either commercial or political risks. The program was revised in mid-1971 to provide for a master policy to cover either all or a negotiated portion of an exporter's sales on credit terms of up to five years. This master policy offers blanket coverage (normally 90 percent) of both commercial and political risks, but it includes a deductible provision for commercial risks to be borne by the exporter himself up to a specified amount called normal loss expectancy. The revised policy also simplified procedures for qualifying individual transactions for insurance coverage, offered blanket political coverage of 70 percent loss from political risks only (without the necessity of insurance against commercial risks), and made special arrangements for small businesses and newcomers to exporting.

Guarantees to Commercial Banks

The American export credit insurance program has been extended to encouraging commercial banks to increase their nonrecourse financing of exporters selling abroad under medium terms (181 days to five years). Under this arrangement the Export-Import Bank will guarantee commercial banks against political risks for early maturities and against both commercial and political risks for later maturities. Commercial banks would assume the commercial risk on the early maturities, since the financing is without recourse on the exporter.

International Coordination of Policies

Just as private companies must compete for business, so must national economies; credit insurers in various countries wish to stay sound and not to outdo each other in simple generosity. Their mutual interest is, as stated by H. T. Aitken, president of Canada's Export Development Corporation, to see that credit is a tool and not a weapon of competition. In order to contribute to rational credit development in the international field, two international associations exist to facilitate cooperation in technical problems and to keep their members informed on developments of common interest.

The first of these is an association of private companies, the International Credit Insurance Association, formed in 1928 and now headquartered in Zurich. As of late 1971 the members, from 22 countries, numbered 31.

In 1934, three private companies and the British Export Credits Guarantee Department founded the Berne Union (Union d'Assurance des Credits Internationaux). Its members include three types of insurers: private insurance companies, private organizations insuring political and possibly commercial risks on behalf of their governments, and government bodies themselves. In its early days it dealt primarily with insurance against commercial risks, but as political risks became more of a problem, the union expanded its relations with government-controlled organizations and private companies offering political risk insurance on behalf of their governments. As of late 1971, there were 28 members from 23 countries. For the United States both the Export-Import Bank and the FCIA are members.

Since some members of the union are not governmental units, the communality of interest is made effective by understandings as to the outside limits of credit coverage. In effect, there is a gentlemen's agreement to avoid excessive international competition in credit terms that call for insurance. The members have agreed to confine their underwriting of credits to five-year maximum maturities except for certain types of aircraft or ships, in which case the credits may run seven years. Members have agreed to notify the Berne Union of their departure from the adopted limits, if there should be any, and probably have to justify such exceptions before their friendly competitors. A danger would seem to be that such exceptions, if numerous or frequent, might make it acceptable for other members to proceed similarly and thus to render them equally competitive on more lenient terms.

In the United States system, the FCIA, countries are classified for operational purposes into groups according to the degree of risks involved; in the weaker ones, the exporter may be required to pay a higher premium and possibly to carry a larger share of the risk. There is, however, no uniformity of country categories by Berne Union members.

The credit insurance programs available to exporters of different countries are not uniform in eligibility criteria nor in compulsory coverage. The result is that, in terms of eligibility, mandatory coverage, commodity makeup, and the destination of a nation's export trade, widely differing proportions of the several countries' exports are insured.

12

Government Participation, Assistance, and Regulation

In the preceding chapters frequent reference was made to government activities related to the conduct of international trade, whether exporting or importing. Some of these activities constitute direct participation in foreign trade, such as the sale of surplus products or direct public procurement from foreign sources for stockpile purposes or for defense or other official responsibilities, either in the United States or abroad. Other activities consist of the provision of numerous services to private exporters or importers, including statistical, commercial, and economic intelligence; direct and indirect trade promotion; financial assistance; and the adoption of policies that offer practical encouragement to and otherwise facilitate export and import efforts by private business.

In order, then, not to repeat unnecessarily the many linkages between government and private business at all levels of international trade, this chapter provides an overview of government attitudes and activities *directly* concerned with international trade. From this it will be evident that all exporting and much importing must be looked on as a privilege and not a right. Unless specifically excluded by regulation, all movements of merchandise into and out of the United States must be disclosed to, and sometimes cleared with, government authorities who are responsible for taxation, statistical requirements, and close control based on considerations such as health and morals, conservation, short supply, unfair trade practices, national security, and the proper conduct of foreign policy.

The Export Control Act of 1949 vests the president with authority to prohibit or curtail the exportation from the United States, its territories, and possessions, of any articles, materials, or supplies, including technical data, except under such rules and regulations as he may prescribe. The Act authorizes him to delegate this authority to such government departments or agencies as he deems appropriate. Imports are subject to acknowledgment to or clearance by government authorities (entry procedures) in all cases, to taxation in many cases (although anyone paying the tax is free to import), and to licensing in some cases. However, positive interdiction or regulation is the exception rather than the rule.

There appears to be a bureaucratic maze in ascertaining the particular executive department or independent agency of the government interested or involved in this or that foreign trade transaction or problem. Frequently it is several, if not many, and in the administration of rules and regulations as well as in the formulation of foreign trade policies, interagency committees and meetings are standard practice. Part of this is a legal requirement, as in the case of escape clause actions or evaluation of adjustment assistance petitions. Recommendations made to the president take into account the views of such departments and agencies as State, Treasury, Commerce, Agriculture, Defense, Interior, Justice, Labor, HEW, and the Tariff Commission.

It is not bureaucratic organization that is most representative of government attitudes, however, or that is of prime interest or most meaning to exporters and importers. It is, instead, government *policy* concerning exports and imports. Such policy is reflected in laws, regulations, and executive branch or independent agency organizational units designed to accomplish the objectives.

In search of broad spectrum coverage of government attitudes, sometimes seemingly at cross purposes, policies may be placed in two broad groupings, restrictive and expansionary. Such direct involvement as there is is primarily related to a legislated policy of restricting or expanding trade (or trade opportunities) either through service to private business or as a regulator thereof. It is not undertaken for profit or other economic goals as such. It is a means to another end rather than an end in itself.

The following outline identifies the principal government policies and activities that constitute its participation in, assistance to, and regulation of the foreign trade of the United States. It is not practicable to include every detail but enough is given to form an adequate basis for appreciating its complexity and for reaching a defensible conclusion as to its net directional thrust, that is, whether the government's attitude is fundamentally one of restricting or of encouraging foreign trade.

U.S. Government Attitudes Toward Foreign Trade

I. Imports
   A. Restrictive policies
      1. Tariffs:
         a. First law passed by Congress was Tariff Act of 1789.
         b. Tariff not always protective; revenue was important in earlier days.
         c. Protectionism became strong about 1815, then went up and down for next 125 years.
         d. The Tariff Act of 1930, with duty rates the highest ever, is still the basic law. However, setting of actual rates is now accomplished by negotiation, with the result that pressure through negotiation is downward.
         e. The Tariff Act provides for valuation (Section 402), for countervailing duties and for drawbacks of duty paid on goods later exported. It also provides for special and additional duties to be applicable under stated conditions.
         f. Other duties or taxes are called for by other legislation, such as Section 22 of the Agricultural Adjustment Act and the Antidumping Act.
      2. Nontariff barriers:
         a. Procurement of domestic goods with public funds, specifically provided for in:
            (1) Buy American Act of 1933.

(2) Defense appropriations (Berry Amendment).
(3) Strategic and Critical Materials Stockpiling Act of 1946.
(4) Merchant Marine Act of 1936.
(5) Federal housing legislation.

b. Marking and labeling requirements.
c. Pure Food and Drug laws (perhaps a barrier but domestic production is subject to the same regulations).
d. Tariff quotas (quasi-nontariff barriers).
e. Quantitative restrictions:
   (1) Section 22 of Agricultural Adjustment Act (tariffs may be used instead of quotas).
   (2) Sugar legislation.
   (3) Cotton Textile Agreement (international agreement).
   (4) Coffee (international agreement).
   (5) Petroleum, oil products, and derivatives.
   (6) About 600 bills calling for import quotas were introduced in the 91st Congress but Congress adjourned in January 1971, without passing any of them.* These varied in methodology but would have restricted imports of many specified products to the level of a preceding period or to a stated share of the U.S. market for the products. In addition, the threat of mandatory, quantitative limits in 1970–1971 induced certain foreign countries to impose "voluntary restraints," in effect controls, on their exports to the United States of products such as textiles, iron, and steel.

B. Expansionary policies
1. Trade Agreements Program:
   a. The original act was passed in 1934 and renewed several times. The latest is the Trade Expansion Act of 1962.
   b. Strong program of negotiations to reduce trade barriers on broad front. Agreements do not call for specific exchanges or barter or preemptive licensing.
   c. Effect on tariff levels:

	1931–1935 Average	*1969*
(1) Duty collections/total imports (%)	18	7
(2) Duty collections/dutiable imports (%)	50	11

   (3) Further reductions scheduled by United States and others under Kennedy Round, phased over five-year period ending in 1972.

   d. Legislation requested in 1970 and 1971, but not passed as of early 1971, would provide for, among other things:
   (1) "Housekeeping authority" to set certain rates in emergency.
   (2) Repeal of American selling price as basis for valuing imports for duty.

* U.S. Department of Commerce, *Commerce Today*, January 11, 1971, p. 48.

(3) Easier access to adjustment assistance provisions of Trade Expansion Act of 1962.
(4) Qualification as Domestic International Sales Corporations, which could defer taxes on income attributable to exports.

e. Customs Simplification Acts of 1954 and 1955.
f. Tariff Classification Act of 1962.
g. Foreign Trade Zones Act of 1934.
h. Automotive Products Trade Act of 1965.

2. Adjustment assistance:
   a. Pinpoints company or worker group experiencing excessive competition from imports; aims at assistance to that entity rather than imposing broad restrictions against importation of product causing difficulty.

II. Exports
   A. Restrictive policies:
      1. Use of export taxes is prohibited by the Constitution
      2. Qualitative controls
         a. Inspection and certification to assure conformity to grade, packaging, and quality for goods moving in foreign commerce:
            (1) Grain Standards Act of 1916.
            (2) Apple and Pear Export Act of 1933.
            (3) Export Grape and Plum Act of 1960.
      3. Quantitative controls:
         a. Export Control Act of 1949 makes all exports subject to control for reasons of:
            (1) National security. Commodity Control List indicates licensing requirements. Licensing may be general or validated; technical data of U.S. origin included.
            (2) Short supply. In recent years control has been invoked to cover beet and cane sugar, walnut logs, copper, nickel scrap, unwrought nickel, and stainless steel scrap.
            (3) Other targets: arms, ammunition, and implements of war; electric energy; gold; narcotics; natural gas; nuclear material; tobacco seeds and plants; and vessels.
   B. Expansionary policies:
      1. Trade agreements program
      2. Automotive Products Trade Act of 1965
      3. International Antidumping Code:
         a. Calls for other countries to require injury to domestic industry in order to impose antidumping duty, as the United States does.
      4. Trade promotion:
         a. Statistical aids.
         b. Reports from Foreign Service posts.
         c. Offices of commercial attachés:
            (1) Development of Trade Lists and World Trade Directory Reports.
            (2) Trade Contact Surveys.

(3) Identification of export and import opportunities.

d. Office of International Trade Promotion:

(1) Fund of commercial intelligence.

(2) Trade centers and trade missions.

e. Offices of agricultural attachés, active in developing market opportunities for agricultural products.

f. Fund of information on foreign trade regulations of and economic conditions in each country, and on international trading conditions and foreign markets for many products, both industrial and agricultural.

g. Joint Export Associations, for which technical and financial assistance is available.

5. Export incentives:

a. Financial facilities:

(1) Rediscountability and open-market purchases of bankers' acceptances.

(2) Export-Import Bank of the United States:
Loans to banks on the basis of their holding export paper.
Guarantees to banks on certain loans related to exports.
Direct loans under certain conditions.

(3) Special agricultural export programs:
Public Law 480.
Commodity Credit Corporation export credit sales program.

(4) Export credit insurance:
Foreign Credit Insurance Association.

(5) Taxation advantages:
Western Hemisphere Trade Corporations.
Domestic International Sales Corporations (proposed, as of early 1971).

6. Environmental efforts:

a. Surveillance of adequacy and nondiscriminatory nature of transportation and communications facilities.

b. Most-favored-nation principle (1923) calling for nondiscrimination in trading opportunities and relations.

(1) United States and other outsiders put to disadvantage in common markets and free trade associations.

(2) Preferences in favor of less-developed countries would negate this principle.

c. Treaties of friendship, commerce, and navigation:

(1) In effect with 44 countries as of early 1971.

(2) Provide freedom of entry and right to engage in business under conditions covered in the treaty.

d. Bilateral and multilateral trade agreements:

(1) Negotiated under reciprocal trade agreements legislation.

(2) Many bilateral agreements superseded by multilateral agreements negotiated under GATT auspices.

e. Participation in multilateral bodies:

(1) General Agreement on Tariffs and Trade (GATT):
Objective is reducing barriers to trade.
Contracting parties as of early 1971 numbered 78 with one provisional accession and 14 other countries applying conditions de facto.
United States applies as executive agreement and not as treaty, so GATT does not contravene national laws.

(2) International Monetary Fund:
Major objective is to facilitate maintenance of stable exchange rates and to provide temporary assistance to members in order to ease pressures on governments that could lead to excessively depressive or restrictive economic policies, especially pertaining to imports.
Articles of agreement (Article 8) prohibit use of exchange controls except when justified by balance of payments considerations.
United States has supported expansion of Fund's resources, including creation of Special Drawing Rights in 1967.

(3) Organization for Economic Cooperation and Development (OECD):
Had roots in Marshall Plan for reconstruction of Europe.
Expanded, and in 1960 the United States became a member via treaty.
Its objective, as far as exports and imports are concerned, is expansion of international trade opportunities, especially by work on nontariff trade barriers, improved statistical intelligence, monetary and fiscal policy coordination, coordination of national policies concerning aid to less-developed countries, and regulation of restrictive business practices.

Index